I Only Know

Know

MY DOUBLE LUNG TRANSPLANT JOURNEY

Ronald Campbell

ADULT
MEMOIR

I ONLY KNOW

MY DOUBLE LUNG TRANSPLANT JOURNEY

Ronald Campbell

ISBN (Print Edition): 978-1-66782-702-5

ISBN (eBook Edition): 978-1-66782-703-2

Library of Congress Control Number: 2021919192

Introduction

This is my story. We all have one, but this is mine. I have decided to tell it not with any grand idea of myself as a sage with all sorts of great wisdom to share. I wanted to share it because one day I'll be gone, and I want my grandkids to know a little more about me, because for those of us who lived through it, it'll be a reminder of hard times and happy days, and because some people might even find parts of it helpful, particularly if they have faced similar obstacles. But be forewarned. I am telling this story from my perspective, the only one I know. If you were part of the story and don't like your parts—write your own book. I have tried to be as honest as possible. Parts of it were hard to write and will be challenging to read. My ultimate hope is that by the time our journey is over, we will have reached a point where we can all look at each other with a touch more empathy. Some names have been changed to protect the innocent. The medical notes and medical verbiage is from MyChart. I felt that you should know that.

Everyone is fighting a battle. This one is mine.

"If our past is all we get to be
my old life would've been the death of me
While I find myself alive, I might as well see where it gets me
I only know I ain't gonna go back"

-Cory Branan

I'm not really sure where to start this whole thing. I don't know if I need to go back to the beginning of my transplant journey or back to the beginning of me. It seems that going all the way back would help to establish who I was and why this journey was such an undertaking. This was a process that impacted everyone in my life, friends and family. I had no idea how much of an impact I would have by simply sharing my struggle. It seems everyone is struggling with so much these days, and my fight helped to provide some encouragement some folks. With that said, let's go all the way back to the beginning. Back to Sanford, NC, circa 1970-something.

I am the product of a small southern town. My parents are products of that same town, as is my wife. My parents met in high school and were married directly after my mom's graduation in 1972: my mom was 17, and my dad had just turned 19. I am an only child, though I was not supposed to be. This feels like a fairly significant part of my story, a part that I'm not sure I have ever really adequately addressed. I'm not sure my family has adequately processed it either. My older brother was born in 1974 and did not survive his birth. I came along in 1976. My younger brother was born in 1982 and, like my older brother, did not survive. I have long struggled with the meaning of these deaths. I can only imagine what they meant to my parents in light of my own health issues. For me, I have never been able to accept my "only-ness." I desperately wanted to have siblings, and it was clear my parents wanted the same. I have asked myself from the beginning why I was the child that survived. It was hard growing up with survivor's guilt for the death of two babies, and I have continued to struggle with it into adulthood. I often think about them. I wish I could've met them. I wonder what kind of people they would have been, who they would have become in the world. I felt cheated out of siblings as a kid; I still do today. It must have been for that reason that I played every part of my childhood just as I was supposed to do. I played sports, became an Eagle Scout, did well in school and stayed out of trouble. The pressure I felt to "do right" was incredible and I feel it to this day.

Still, for the most part my childhood proceeded with a more or less normal rhythm. School, sports, summer vacations, the occasional trip to Disney World—all the things that mark childhood. I do remember feeling from an early age that there was some difference between myself and the rest of my family. My dad's parents lived next door to us and were typical Southern folks of a particular generation. Being a member of that generation brought with it lots of baggage: baggage and prejudice that I saw firsthand on many occasions. Sometimes I saw it directed toward my mom. Even though she was born in my hometown, my mom was the product of war refugees. Her parents and several of her siblings had spent time in concentration camps during World War II and hopped around Europe through the late 1940s. In the early '50s they made their way to the United States and eventually settled in my hometown. There weren't many Polish Catholics in my small southern town back then, and they could feel the stares and judgment. It was a real issue for my WASP grandparents when my dad started dating my mom. I'm not altogether sure my grandparents ever really accepted my mom.

As a result, I always felt a bit on the outside when it came to my grandparents, isolated and lonely. I had cousins, some of whom lived nearby, but I always felt somehow removed from them too. I was a bit older, but it was more than just that. It was a feeling of disconnect, like I didn't fit in. My parents, on the other hand, were fully invested in my childhood. They tried their best to make me feel included. It was a noble effort. Maybe my family never meant to make me feel excluded, but it was still how I felt.

I think because of what my mom faced, I grew up a little more tolerant of other folks. It's really only been in the past few years that I've started to recognize this as the beginning of what I call a Southern Renaissance. There are lots of us who recognize the need for a better south. I look back on my childhood, and I can vividly remember saying and doing things that now make me cringe. It just seemed acceptable at the time, but it wasn't acceptable then and it isn't acceptable now. I am somewhat ashamed of some of those things, and I am trying hard now to be "better." After graduating from Lee Senior High School in June of 1995, I went to UNC Chapel Hill. There my horizons continued to expand. I met people from all over, attended class with them, lived with them, learned from them. College was fantastic. From either an educational or social perspective it could not have been better. The problem was that I was never really focused on what I would do when I graduated.

I say all of this to point out that while my childhood was more or less normal (as these things go), there were parts that always made me feel a bit different. I was smaller than most of my friends, I had a sense of humor that seemed to go over some folks' heads, I had a touch of a mouth on me, and I was kinda smart. All together these were parts of my childhood that made me work harder for acceptance. Parts that made me work harder to be successful. Parts that developed my wit and humor as a defense mechanism. Parts that made me look outside of my small little world for greater meaning. Parts that would prove vital as I took this journey of transplant.

My family

After college I got married to my high school girlfriend, Erin, on June 12, 1999. We were young. Not as young as my parents, but still maybe too young. I was clearly not experienced enough in life for her to take a chance on. I didn't know what I wanted to do or where my life was going, I just knew I wanted her to be a part of it. I think her parents felt a twinge of concern and weren't sure she should take the leap on me. To this day, part of me believes she could've done better, and to this day, I'm not sure why she sticks around. As we follow this journey, her impact will become clear. Her importance to me is immeasurable.

We began life together as two kids at the close of the twentieth century. We were both working entry-level jobs that we'd leave in due time and were trying to figure out how to be married. We were broke but fairly happy. Then our circumstances changed. I'll never forget it. It was in late May 2002. We were driving in our hometown. Erin was acting odd, and I made an off-hand joke about her "being pregnant or something." As it turned out, she was. You could've knocked me over with a feather. I feel confident I did some of my best driving in that moment by managing to not crash the car. We were still very young, still very broke, and still very much trying to figure each other out, and now we were going to be parents. People often talk about waiting for "the right time" to have kids. I have come to believe there is no such thing as the right time. They come when they come, ready or not. I am also convinced that so many of these unexpected events in my life have helped to prepare me for this fight I am in right now.

We prepared for a baby. On January 22, 2003 our daughter Emma was born at Rex Hospital in Raleigh. Going to the hospital that morning, we didn't know what we were having. I didn't care. As long as my wife and new child were fine, I would be OK. Erin had been scheduled for an induction, which seemed to give us some semblance of control over the situation. We had even been able to stop off and get me a bagel and coffee on the way: a sesame bagel with bacon scallion cream cheese. To this day, it is a requirement that someone in the house eat this very thing on her birthday. We call it the "Emma Special." By mid-afternoon, Emma had been born. I didn't get to cut the umbilical cord as it was wrapped around her neck, but I didn't care. The doctor's handled this small detail and she was just fine.

We quickly started to figure out this little person's idiosyncrasies and personality, and she ours. We learned early on that she did not like to be swaddled or constrained in any way (and she still doesn't). Emma's eyes were bright, and from the very beginning she seemed to be absorbing everything. I remember bringing her home for the first time. I was so nervous on the drive from Raleigh to Sanford. Everyone else on the road seemed to be in a race. We brought her inside and placed her where our dog, Scooter, could have a sniff. He seemed to approve. I really felt like things were not in my control any longer and that I would have to learn how to adapt to ever-changing situations. It's still a work in progress, but it had to start somewhere.

We moved from Sanford to Cary when Emma was six months old, and Erin returned to work full time around that same time. One day I was home alone with Emma and she was crying uncontrollably, and nothing I did was working. I didn't know what to do, so I called Erin. This was a mistake. She told me to figure it out and not to call back. Tough love, but good advice. I looked at Emma, made sure she was safe, told her I loved her, and then closed the door and walked out of the room. Eventually, she settled down and stopped crying. Sometimes you can't "fix" a situation directly. Sometimes walking away is the best option. And sometimes you just need to cry it out.

And so our little family settled in to our little house and our little routines. Erin was back at work full time, and by the end of the summer, I was back to teaching. Eventually Emma was in day care. We didn't have tons of money, but like everyone says, they were good times. There were many tuna casseroles for dinner, and we were working to stretch every dollar. I don't remember Emma's first word, her first step, or those sort of "milestones" that everyone says you'll never forget. Well, I forgot 'em. What I do remember are the times she and I spent together after school and on school breaks. I remember picking her up from preschool and visiting Fresh Market for a "fancy drink." Really it was just a soft drink in a glass bottle, but she thought she was high class, and I felt high class for being able to provide such an extravagance. Some days I'd take her to her favorite restaurant, "Chick o Lay" (Chick-fil-A), we'd eat, and she'd play on the playground. One time we took her to Disney World a month or two before she turned three: our motto was, "She's free till she's three." It helped that she also didn't realize that the stuff in the gift shops was for sale. She was perfectly happy to play with a toy for a minute and put it back. Saved us a ton! Emma has always been a confident young lady, and this trait will serve her well. This was our life, and it was good. As it tends to do, however, time marched on.

In June 2006, we were lucky enough to be graced with the presence of another daughter. Her arrival was a doozey. Erin started labor around six in the morning, and by ten, Rachel was here. I drove to the hospital the way it's portrayed in movies, like Ricky Bobby: "I wanna go fast." Actually, I had to go fast. Rachel was on her way. I dropped Erin at the door, and by the time I parked and got back, she was ready to push. Rachel was also born with her umbilical cord around her neck. Unlike her sister, she didn't breathe for a couple of minutes. It felt like hours. Eventually, she took that first breath and let out a wail. She would be fine. The nurse took us to the nursery. While we were gone, Erin's mom got to the hospital and was shocked that we were already done.

I was definitely more confident this time around. I don't remember Rachel's "milestones" either. I do remember being able to calm her down when no one else could (still true). I would put my forehead to hers and calmly talk to her. It worked every time. While I no longer put my head to hers, I can still talk her down. I remember watching her grow into her very quirky personality. There are photos of her that still make me laugh. I remember kicking a soccer ball with her and being shocked at how strong she was. Mostly, I just remember being there with them. Everyone makes such a big deal about certain things being so important. I'm not sure the specifics really matter. Sure, it'd be nice to remember a first step, or word, or something like that. But what I remember, and what I hope they remember, is just being with each other. As I've gone through this process, there have been moments that I am sure I will forget. What I won't forget is how my girls were there for me. Without them, I'm not sure I would've survived.

So there you have it. Our family was complete, and we settled in for their childhoods. We moved to Raleigh in 2007. Jobs were changed, schools started and finished. I used to love picking Rachel up and then waiting for Emma to get off of the school bus. Walking home with my girls, sometimes they'd even hold my hand. It made me burst with happiness.

I do believe that I have succeeded in instilling in my kids a love of travel. Travel, for me, was the one way I could escape my little town and broaden my horizons. There were beach trips, the occasional trip to Disney World, and one time I went out west for a month. I was the kid who would call 1-800 numbers for travel guides to faraway places. Places like Maine! Arkansas! Delaware! Woo boy! Looking back, my parents couldn't afford extravagant trips. The trips to Disney World probably broke them. For us, providing our children with experiences and not material goods has been important. I wanted them to get out there and do. My parents tried to give me all they could back in those days. The greatest gift they ever gave me was the gift of experiences. One in particular stands out. In the Summer of 1993 I was able to participate in Teens Westward Bound. This 23 day trip around the American West was transformative. I saw firsthand how beautiful our country is. I learned to travel with people I didn't know. I learned how to live each day to the max. I learned not to care about the opinions of others:

I'd probably never see those "tourists" again, so who cares? Each sunrise, each new vista was a gift. At the end of it all, our experiences are all that we will carry with us.

When I was at my lowest points in my decline, I could always close my eyes and go back on some of those trips. I might not know where a t-shirt or some souvenir would end up, but I could always travel back to a place and feel that feeling again. I could see my kids as little girls again. Going back on these trips and thinking of future ones really did help keep me going. I didn't want my girls to stop having memories of me when they were 18 and 14 (almost 15). We traveled to lots of cool spots. We took cruises when they were young because they were an easy way to get out there and gently expose them to other places. We've tubed in Jamaica, explored an underground river in Playa del Carmen, swam with stingrays in Grand Cayman. We have surfed in Hanalei, hiked part of the Kalalau Trail, been to Pearl Harbor. I've taken them to the Grand Canyon, Yosemite, Zion, Arches, San Francisco, the Pacific Coast Highway, and Alaska.

We have more planned and we will get there. Someday. Back in January of 2021 I honestly didn't know if I would see February. Now, I can look forward. It's an odd thing, now. Looking back at those pictures I smile at the memories they bring. But I wonder now, was I dying in those photos? When did I start to get sick? I suppose it's immaterial. What I really wanted was for my kids to see their country and fall in love with its beauty. I've tried to whet their appetites so as they move on their own, they will continue to explore and be curious. Being curious about the world around you pays off not only in expanding your understanding, but in teaching you to ask questions. Being willing to learn helps you in everyday life. Standing where history happened is an exciting thing. I am certain I keep asking questions that the doctors rarely get. Questions are good. Learning is good. Being willing to accept that there are multiple ways to achieve a common goal is crucial. Travel intensifies everything. It makes you question things, makes you learn, and it forces you out of your comfort zone. All of this would prove useful as I navigated this journey.

So, I guess that's me. I didn't cover my deep and undying love of music and my willingness to travel all over to see a band, how much music sustains me and how I get weepy over certain songs. I didn't mention playing drums, and now guitar. It will be obvious that music is one of the most important things in my life. But we'll learn more as I unspool this thread.

I am a sum of all of my experiences—good and bad. We all are. We all come to the table with our struggles. Meeting folks where they are and not where we want or expect them to be matters. I am the son of southern parents from a small southern town. I am the grandson of privileged folks and the grandson of Holocaust survivors. I am an only child with two brothers who never got to follow their dreams or even take a breath. I carry all of this baggage every day. I am the husband to a wife who, despite all of my shortcomings, sticks around. I am the father of two daughters who make my life worth fighting for. I am a traveler and a seeker. I am a double lung transplant survivor. And so, my journey begins.

———————

My childhood would be considered normal by most people. Yet for as normal as it appeared, there seemed to always be medical issues that needed attention. I'm not altogether sure what the genesis of these issues was. Was there some event that precipitated all of my mom's concerns? Was my mom overly cautious about any perceived threat to me out of an abundance of caution? Was I really sickly? Was the memory of losing two sons so strong that any sniffle caused a trip to the doctor? I'm not sure. I don't remember ever being all that sick. I do remember being told that there was something wrong with my lungs. I remember going to UNC Hospitals and blowing into some device and trying to keep a ping pong ball aloft (how very early '80s). My mom was also concerned that I didn't seem to be growing much. Apparently, I was a runt. Still am. While I'm still hoping for a growth spurt,

I'm closing in on resigning myself to my destiny to be on the smaller size. I'll never be one of those "tall, dark, and handsome" types.

The one true medical concern that I actually have vivid memories of struggling with was my juvenile rheumatoid arthritis. My body seems to gravitate toward auto-immune diseases. The JRA manifested itself fairly early in my life and would often announce itself by stiffening my joints to the point where just flexing my fingers was impossible. I would truly "lock up," unable to move. It sucked. I didn't feel like anyone understood the pain I was experiencing on a daily basis. My dad adopted a "walk it out" philosophy. He seemed to think that if I was stiff, I just needed to work the joints loose. He didn't understand how painful it was. And I was eight. I came to learn at an early age that my pain was just that: mine. No one could understand it; I alone had to deal with it.

I don't know the date, but for some reason, at some point in my adolescence, the JRA just sorta went away. I would assume it was sometime around puberty. For whatever reason and in whatever fashion, it was gone, and I was pain-free. I had been raised as a typical kid, but in a protective bubble. I can't fault my parents. Coming off of the heartbreak of burying two sons, I'm sure every ache or sneeze or wheeze prompted them, particularly my mom, to launch into medical mode. Looking back on it now, I think I was picking up some skills that would prove invaluable as my current struggles began. My mom was a fierce advocate for me. She fought relentlessly to try to get me access to care that might help me. But I was simply a victim of my era. It was the late 1970s and early '80s. At that point, the doctors might as well have told me to "rub some dirt on it." I think my issues, minor or not, were just more than the medical science of the times could handle. Another side effect of dealing with some of these issues was that I developed a pretty high pain threshold, as well as a tenacity to not let any of this deter me from accomplishing what I wanted. I played baseball, played drums (if you could call it that), and was basically a typical teen.

My high school years passed pain- and issue-free (medically speaking) and I went to college. I did start to notice as a member of the Marching Tar Heels that my hands would start to get a bit tight. I just brushed it off as a side effect of drum practice. I had to practice: I was the absolute weakest member of the snare line my sophomore and junior years. It wasn't even close. I struggled to keep up and was in constant awe of the skills of those around me. One season, I was placed between the two tallest snare players. To this day, I'm convinced that the drum instructor hoped I'd simply disappear between these two awesome players and he could forget I was there. I was never going to equal their skill: I was simply not as talented as them. But I would not be discouraged. I could work hard, and I did work hard, to be as good as I could be. As monotonous and boring as the practice cold sometimes be, it was absolutely essential. It made be better on game day. Much like in rehab many years later, I had to put in the hard work. No one forced me, but I knew it would have an impact on the outcome. The hard work often left my hands tired. Again, this seemed normal and reasonable, and once the season was over, things more or less settled down.

Putting in the hard work to be successful was something that would prove vital on my journey. One of the biggest lessons in the importance of hard work for the simple outcome of achieving a goal without fanfare came in the summer of 1997. That summer was one of the best of my life, spent as a member of the Walt Disney World College Program—with my head in the trash as a Custodial Host in the Magic Kingdom. You wanna do something thankless, hard, and without glory? Empty trash and sweep streets in Central Florida in the summer. Woo. It was hot and smelly work, but it had to be done, and I loved every minute of it. I met folks from all over the United States, all over the world. I lived in an apartment complex full of college students and the different countries Cultural Representatives in EPCOT. Eye-opening is one way to describe it. Each day was filled with new experiences and fun. We made sweeping Main Street, USA into a game. We made a ball out of tape and played street hockey with kids using our pans and brooms as sticks. I became quite adept at trick shots with that equipment. We worked—sorta. Mostly we learned what it meant to truly enjoy yourself. Being assigned to work as a custodian could have been a bad job. Like most things in life, it was what you made it.

When I went to college, I went for the purpose of achieving some high-flying career. That summer, I also learned that it was more important to do a job you could be proud of, and pay be damned. I made minimum wage ($5.35/hr in those days) and came home with about 50 bucks at the end of the experience. The lessons I learned, though, were worth a mint. I learned that being self-motivated to just "do the work" and be proud of what you accomplished matters. And yes, you'll sweep the same damn street one thousand times and empty those freakin' Hub trash cans dozens of times. It's gotta get done. You can't shirk the responsibility of doing your job. It's not glorious but it is essential. As we progress in my struggle, there will be things that happened that were glorious (and I'll tell you about them) and other things that were not glorious, but were essential (I'll tell you about those too). I don't know how it is there now, but then, at the end of the twentieth century, the way I emptied trash cans was by pushing a huge cart down Main Street and stopping at each bin to dump it. Often, I was going against the flow of the crowd. Getting folks to move was hard, and sometimes I needed help. It was OK to ask for that help. I also developed more of a sense of humor that summer, because sometimes that was the only way to deal with the tourists. Sometimes, now, humor is the only way to deal with my transplant. If I can't laugh, I may cry. In life, there is room for both.

My time at UNC came to a close with Commencement in December of 1998. I graduated a semester early (one of the first of many errors I would commit moving forward). I got a job and moved to Charlotte while preparing for our June 1999 wedding. I left that job at the end of May because they were unwilling to work with my new bride. They suggested I tell her to get a job waiting tables, implying that my job was so great I should tell my new, super-intelligent wife to put her career goals on hold. I told them goodbye and cast my lot with her. That was a great call on my part. For the rest of 1999 through the summer of 2001, I bounced around a couple of jobs trying to find my place. I worked for the Boy Scouts and even tried to sell insurance. Eventually I found my way in front of a classroom teaching history. I loved every second of it, and I was good at it. I taught in Lee County for a year and then moved to Wake County in 2002. I started out teaching eighth graders during that one year at West Lee Middle and then two years at Apex Middle. After three years teaching middle school, I moved on to teach AP European History at Apex High, and I could not have been happier. I loved the curriculum; I loved the humor of the high school kids. I should have just stayed put.

I had an administrator who saw me teaching and suggested that I become an administrator. Her argument was that as an administrator, I could impact an entire school. As a teacher, I could only impact the small number of kids in my classes. As I've grown older, this differentiation between impacting an individual versus impacting a more "global" community has become an interesting dynamic to ponder. Just like writing all of this. Am I impacting a larger group or is my impact smaller? Does it matter? Back then, I was just too young to understand this. So I then made the huge mistake of getting a Master's Degree in School Administration and becoming an assistant principal at an elementary school that will remain nameless in perpetuity. It was a terrible situation from the very start and it was clear that I had made an error. I thought that moving on and up in a career was what was expected. I was wrong. Leaving the classroom was the single biggest career mistake I made in my life and one that I continue to regret. I forgot the lessons of the summer of 1997 and chased the dollar and "glory" that came with promotion. If I had remembered my hard knocks from that summer, I'd have stayed put and been content.

It was in that second year at Apex Middle that I started to notice that I was having some real issues with my gut. It seemed that, at certain times and after eating certain things, I just couldn't keep things in. I often had to run out of the class to visit the restroom. My weight was dropping, and my stomach was frequently distended. By the time I left the school system altogether, to work for the City of Raleigh in 2007, I was down in the 130s. I realize I'm not a big guy, but that was low. Even for runt standards. I made Barney Fife look like The Rock. It was also around that time that my joint pain returned, and with a vengeance. There were days when I couldn't make a fist and walking was next to impossible. It's kind of weird to believe, but my kids have never known me to not hurt. That's sad.

Were my joint pain and stomach issues linked? Who knew? Because I had a history with the rheumatology folks at UNC Hospitals from my JRA days, and because my mom was working there as a nurse, she was able to help secure me an appointment with the rheumatology clinic. It took some time, but on October 29, 2003 I got in and spent the better part of the afternoon at the clinic. I was x-rayed, and my mom helped me to present my history. It was fairly early that the doctor told me that my JRA was back and that now it was just good ol' rheumatoid arthritis. I guess I had aged out from the "juvenile" part. So now I was fully diagnosed with a real, adult auto-immune disease. From 2003–2012 I saw the same doctor and was prescribed every medicine possible to treat RA, no matter how new or painful. If you've seen a commercial for an RA medicine, from pill to infusion, I've had it. I thought the RA would be the end of all of this. I mean, it was enough, right? Everybody has something, so I figured this was mine. I've seen folks with mangled hands, heard of people who died from complications related to the RA. This shit can mess with your heart!

Among other organs.

But hey, it's only one disease—we can manage it. And we did. I took my medicines as prescribed, exercised, tried to eat right. But still I couldn't put on weight, and I was still sick in my gut much of the time. Erin and I went to Vegas in January of 2012, and I spent every night sleeping on the bathroom floor. I was sick as a dog, and unlike most visitors to Vegas, it wasn't related to over-consumption. That whole year I was sick. My doctor left the rheumatology clinic and I was adrift. I visited an urgent care and they put me on a BRAT diet—Bananas, Rice, Applesauce, and Toast—to try and clear up my stomach issues. It didn't help. Eventually, I found a primary care doctor and managed to get a referral to a gastroenterologist. After having an upper and lower GI endoscopy performed (upper first, and be sure to wash the scope), it was established that I had celiac disease. Well, smack my fanny and call me Sally. I now have two, count 'em, two, auto-immune diseases. Man, I tell ya. I don't futz around do I? My diet was altered, and what do you know? I started to gain weight and not be sick all the damn time. And now, when I got sick, I knew why. It also explained Vegas and many other nights in the bathroom over the past few years. OK, so now that's two "things." I was telling the universe that I had met my quota for medical issues.

But for me, it raised another question: Why does this keep happening? I tried to be good. I tried to live right and follow my doctor's advice, but it felt like I had a black cloud over my head. I didn't smoke. I ate pretty well. I exercised. It just felt unfair. I realize these two issues are manageable. Medicine and exercise can manage the RA, and diet can manage the celiac, but I just felt piled on. I was tired of having activities limited by joint pain and diet limited by, well, vomit. Once I got the celiac diagnosis in January 2013, things did improve, and we felt we had everything well in hand. Really, from 2013-2019 we were right. I felt pretty good. I was seeing a new rheumatologist who kept putting me on every medicine on the market, and I was keeping food down—for the most part. It was challenging on some levels. We could no longer be spontaneous in dining out. Vacations required research and restaurant reservations. Had this been my childhood, I'd have been screwed. Now, though, I was able to use apps, the web, so many resources. Was it challenging? Sure, but it was doable. And we did it. In my years after celiac (AC), we've traveled to Hawaii, around the desert Southwest, California, Alaska, Utah, New York, and Boston, among other places. We didn't let my auto-immune issues limit our family. We just kept on living.

It's in Boston that we pick up the thread of my lungs.

In May 2019 I made my way to Boston with Erin and two of our best friends for a music festival. The trip had been planned for almost a year, and all of us were excited to make the trip. This was my third trip to the town, and I really did dig coming here. It's eminently walkable, the people are nice enough and the history oozes out of every corner: a historical marker, the grave of some famous founding American, a battle site, whatever. There's lots to see and do. The dining scene is great and there are enough Irish pubs that I'm not sure one could ever get to them all. We especially enjoy going with one of our friends as she is Irish and brings a fantastic perspective to every pub we enter. On this particular trip, she actually had friends in common with the Uber driver who took us from the airport to the hotel. Apparently they ran in similar circles in Ireland. We had tickets to Lost Evenings III at the House of Blues, a music festival put on by one of my favorite artists, Frank Turner, a folk/punk singer from England. He's great. I dig his lyrics, his stage presence, and his overall vibe. My friend Tupper turned me on to him several years ago, and we've never looked back. Tupper and I (with our wives) have traveled all over to see him and his band, The Sleeping Souls. We've seen them in Vegas, Charlottesville, Red Rocks, Charlotte, and Boston once before this 2019 trip. Obviously, since this was Lost Evenings III, there had been two others. Those were held in London, so clearly harder to get to. But Boston, hey, we can do that! We bought our tickets for all four days of the event for us, and for two nights for our wives. Sprinkled amid the music were trips around Boston and some great dining.

I learned something about myself on this trip. I'm too old for music festivals. I mean, I loved every second of the shows. All the bands were great, the venue was awesome, and the company even better. But hoo boy, standing for four nights for hours on end—that was not easy. Especially after having toured around during the day. At this point, you might be thinking, "I thought you were going to mention your lungs…" Well, OK. Here ya go. As I was standing and dancing and generally making merry at the shows, I noticed that for some reason I was getting really winded. Not so much that I couldn't breathe, it was just a bit noticeable. I chalked it up to really enjoying myself. As we walked through Boston, I noticed that stairs were really making me wheeze too, so much so that Tupper suggested I do a little more cardio when I got home to try and improve my stamina. We laughed it off and I really didn't give it too much thought while we were there. It was enough of a concern that I made a mental note to mention it to my rheumatologist at my next appointment, though. Given my medical history, it just seemed prudent.

And I mentioned it. I told her that I was having trouble breathing upon exertion, and she suggested I mention it to my primary care doctor. So, I made an appointment and revisited this with him. At the close of 2018 he had already prescribed a rescue inhaler. As a kid, there had been discussion of me having exercise-induced asthma. His suggestion at this visit was that I lose a few pounds and keep using the inhaler.

Months pass and nothing improves. In fact, I begin to notice that I am actually having more and more difficulty. Again, I mention it to my rheumatologist. Again, she says to mention it to my primary care. Again I do, again I'm told to lose a few pounds. I mean, at this point, I'm in some type of endless loop. One doctor is passing the buck (I'm looking at you, rheumatologist), and the other is doing the bare minimum. Neither one of them seems to want to actually address the problem.

It should be noted that yes, losing a couple of pounds would not have been the worst thing, but I wasn't exactly a candidate for weight loss surgery. I really felt like I wasn't being taken seriously. In fact, the records that I obtained from my rheumatologist don't even mention the concern until Fall of 2019. On that I call bull shit. I mentioned it before and was clearly dismissed. I would testify to this in court. I told her, but she was dismissive. The primary care doctor was equally useless. This is where the lessons I learned from my mom started to come in handy. I started to become a very vocal advocate for myself. By the time I had made up my mind to schedule another appointment with my primary care for a referral, 2020 had begun. We didn't know it at the time, but that trip to Boston would be our last vacation for over two years. As it turned out, it could've been my last vacation ever.

We all remember 2020, right? The year that was going to be great? All of the cool weekend holidays lined up? We had planned to take an extended trip to Italy. Emma was going to start her senior year, and Rachel was going to start high school. They'd be together for the first time in years. Everything was going to be just great. The year started with promise. Rachel was captain of her school basketball team and even though they weren't exactly world-beaters, they were a great group of kids. I enjoyed being around them and doing the scoreboard at home games. It was fun, and a great way to be engaged in the game without become too "involved." I had decided to return to school to pick up a two-year degree in radiography. To do this, I would have to complete two prerequisites. I needed to take a math class (as it had been more than 10 years since my last one) and an anatomy class. I went to class two days a week and then usually worked the scoreboard once or twice a week. I loved being able to be a part of this time in Rachel's life. Emma, on the other hand, was cruising through her junior year. She was getting great grades, her band season in the fall had been great (though long—the football team made the state championship game), and everything was just fine. Erin was working as hard as ever and tax season was yet again drawing near. It was a routine we were used to. Yeah, I was still having some trouble walking up steps, but I figured I'd get that checked out and we'd move on down the road. Heck, our trip to Italy was only a few short months away.

The first rumblings of something odd happening in the world began around Christmas of 2019. There was a virus in China that was impacting lungs, and it seemed to be highly contagious. Here in the US we were still just moving on with life, however. Erin went to a conference in Texas in late January, and we took a weekend trip to Beaufort in mid-February. On that trip Erin started to feel unwell and when we got home the doctor told her that she had pneumonia. She did not have pneumonia. March 13 is the day that it all came to an end for our kids. Schools were closing, people were working from home, and toilet paper was unavailable. COVID-19 had been declared a global pandemic and would be just one more challenge that we, along with everyone else, had to face. By the time we got to May of 2020, our kids were doing remote learning, Erin was working at home, and all of our summer plans had been canceled. Like the rest of the planet, we were fairly isolated, only venturing out for groceries and the occasional driveway meetup. By May, my breathing had gotten so labored that I called the primary care doctor and scheduled another appointment. This time, I would refuse to leave until I had a referral to a pulmonologist. I went for my visit in June. The visit went something like this:

I'm called back to the examination room and vitals are taken.

"What is the purpose of your visit?" the nurse asks.

"I'm still having trouble with breathing, two years later," I say.

The doctor eventually enters and listens to my lungs.

"There seems to be something going on in there. Let's get some x-rays and I'll give you an albuterol treatment and we'll re-evaluate," he says.

I think to myself, "Something going on in there? No shit, I've been saying that for a couple of years now."

X-rays are taken and albuterol administered. The doctor comes back in and listens again to my lungs.

"Well, the albuterol didn't seem to do anything, and the x-rays did show some abnormalities," the doctor tells me. I keep thinking that this is nothing new and I am not in the least surprised. I begin to wonder what medical school this yahoo attended and if "practicing medicine" is more than just an expression for him. I could have told him all of these things based on my anecdotal experiences, but I guess he needs clinical proof. It's also worth noting that I am having issues with my lungs in the middle of a pandemic of a virus that affects the lungs. Good timing, huh? But whaddya know, I get the referral to a pulmonologist with Rex/UNC Health Care. This will end up being a big step forward in the lengthy process to get some traction.

So here we were, a couple of years into a process to figure out what is wrong with me. Repeated brush offs by primary care physicians. A rheumatologist that continued to pass the buck. But finally, a referral to someone who might, just might, be able to provide some insight and perhaps relief. Heck, maybe I'd even get fixed. It was early June when the visit to primary care happened. My visit to the pulmonologist wouldn't occur until late August. I would have to go through the entire summer of 2020 wondering what was wrong, and all the while getting steadily worse. I could feel myself getting sicker (for lack of a better word). It started to get to the point where everything was leaving me winded. Walking to the mailbox, mowing the lawn, even just walking down some stairs at our local pool would leave me gasping. I had also developed a dry, unproductive cough that was a killer and would hit me when I exerted effort. Once I sat for a bit, I'd be OK-ish, but as we got closer to the end of summer, I was beginning to have difficulty just having a conversation. I'd get winded talking. Everyone found this refreshing initially, as they were finally able to get a word in, but I think my struggles began to make folks nervous. The pandemic was moving on, and things were opening up a little more. People were beginning to reemerge from their homes and live again. While this was great for everyone else, I was starting to feel more and more restricted.

August arrived, and we began to prepare for Emma's senior year and Rachel's freshman year. It would not be a typical one. For any of us. They would begin these important years remotely, trying to navigate the ups and downs on a computer screen. I was trying to help them as best as I could, but as the fall progressed, they would end up being the ones who helped me. And so the school year began, and Erin and I went to the pulmonologist associated with Rex/UNC Health.

Eventually, we'll need to break down events on a week-to-week or even day-to-day basis. But for now, month-to-month will do. Buckle up, things are gonna get weird—and fast.

August 2020

My first appointment with an actual pulmonologist occurred on August 6, 2020. For the first time in this entire odyssey, someone was listening to me. The doctor was finally engaged and actually had a freaking clue what to do. He took some time to listen to my history, asked me some questions, and then listened to my lungs. At the end of his diagnostics, he made a pronouncement.

"I think you have interstitial lung disease," he proclaimed, "but I want to do someone tests to confirm. We'll need to do some more x-rays, a CT scan, and a pulmonary function test, with a six minute walk. That will give me a good idea of what to do next. If we confirm it to be ILD, we can try to treat it with medicine, though it is progressive and the only true fix is a potential transplant. I'll also refer you to an ILD specialist at UNC Hospitals."

"Great," I said. "Just tell me what to do." Erin and I left the doctor that day with some sense of direction and purpose. It was amazing what having an actual diagnosis meant to me. I felt validated. It might seem like a simple thing, but it made the years of struggle make sense. We also had hope that things could get better. In all honesty, I was shaken by the word "transplant." It was the first time I had heard this mentioned and it wasn't something we'd expected. Erin immediately pointed out the fact that he'd said we could try and treat it with medicines. My after-visit plan that day required me to get lab work done, some imaging, and a breathing test. The doctor would contact my rheumatologist and discuss my current medicines. My next appointment at this office would be with the Physician's Assistant, one month later. As I waited for that month to pass, I would get the imaging done, and continue to worsen.

September 2020

O n September 3, I returned to meet with the PA at Rex. It's funny to me now, looking back. I thought I was so sick at the time, and I was, but boy, if I knew then how bad it would get…

My vital signs from that day are interesting for sure. My weight was a whopping 183 pounds. 183, for crying out loud! By the time this was over, my lowest would be 156. I would lose almost 30 pounds in this process. Anyway, I'm getting ahead of myself. My blood pressure was 139/94 and my oxygen saturation was 96%. The PA was friendly and genuinely concerned about my health. Again I felt like I had an advocate in this process. I was no longer fighting alone. I would see the doctor again soon, but not before getting the pulmonary function test done. The PA also thought it would be a good idea to do an overnight study of my oxygen perfusion to see how I was doing while I slept. I was on board with this, though I'm not sure I was ready for where this would all take me.

I returned to see the PA on September 16 for what would be a fairly significant appointment. We really had no idea how bad things were getting with me until this appointment and it wasn't until I read the notes in my chart that I now understand how sick I was getting. As we moved through this process I have learned more about lungs than I ever wanted to know. One benefit of having taken the anatomy class in the spring is that I at least had a cursory understanding. I would be taking the class of a lifetime as fall became winter. The PA went over my CT Scan with me. It indicated ILD and mildly enlarged mediastinal lymph nodes.

I guess now is as good as a time as any to explain interstitial lung disease. According to the Cleveland Clinic:

> Interstitial lung disease (ILD) is another term for pulmonary fibrosis, which means "scarring" and "inflammation" of the interstitium (the tissue that surrounds the lung's air sacs, blood vessels and airways). This scarring makes the lung tissue stiff, which can make breathing difficult. ILD may be limited to the lung, or it can be related to a condition that may affect other parts of the body, such as **rheumatoid arthritis** or **sarcoidosis**.
>
> These illnesses share similar features, including a nonproductive (dry) cough and shortness of breath. Although they may look similar radiographically (on **chest x-ray** or chest **CT scan**), ILDs from different causes and conditions have different treatments and outlooks. ILD is more common in adults, but can rarely occur occurs in children."

Hold up! Does that say it can be related to another condition such as rheumatoid arthritis?? Didn't I mention all of this to my rheumatologist? Shouldn't a so-called specialist in a field be able to piece together this mystery? Am I right to be this pissed? At every visit to the primary care and rheumatologist over the past two years, I basically described my symptoms from the second paragraph verbatim. Why did no doctor listen?!? Not for the first time in this journey —and nor would it be the last—I was angry. I was angry that I had been ignored. I was angry that things had progressed to this point. I would have to learn how to process my anger in a way that would not be harmful. This would prove to be one of my greatest challenges.

Back to the appointment. I had some pulmonary function tests performed this morning before I met with the PA. These tests involved me breathing into a machine as hard as I could until the therapist told me to stop. There were several variations, but the one that I would come to be the most familiar with centered around me breathing normally for two or three cycles, taking as big of a breath as possible, and then exhaling as hard and for as long as I could. These first rounds of testing showed that my FEV1 was 42% and my FVC was 47%. This netted me an overall lung function of 41%. The FEV1 number will be important as I go along, but they all matter. FEV1 is forced expiratory volume, the amount of air you can force out in the first second of the test. The FVC, or forced vital capacity, is the total amount of air you're able to expel. You take these numbers together to get your overall lung function. At this point, I was operating at 41% of my overall capacity, less than half of what they should. This went a long, long way in explaining why I was so damn short of breath. The results from my ambulatory test, which involved walking back and forth for six minutes, showed that my oxygen levels would desaturate to 88%. This is not good either, and the overnight test they had ordered showed desaturation as well as borderline hypoxia. I was placed on overnight oxygen at this point and would be tethered to oxygen for part of every day for the next several months.

Erin and I left this appointment in a down mood. Especially me. I guess I shouldn't really speak for how she felt. I don't know that I was ever really sure how she felt about all of this. She's a taskmaster, and her focus immediately shifted to working through the problem. She never allowed herself, at least with me, to address the emotional impact this was having. I mean, I was moving on to what the next steps would be too, but I think the difference is that I was beginning to realize that what I was facing could ultimately kill me. Two months shy of turning 44, I wasn't ready to confront my mortality, but like everything else over the past year, I was being confronted with something that was out of my hands and something that we'd just have to face on a day to day basis.

It's September 29 now, and I am seeing the ILD specialist. Reviewing my chart from my first visit to the ILD specialist is like trying to decipher hieroglyphics without the benefit of the Rosetta Stone. Here's the basic takeaway: I'm sick, and he's going to be aggressive because of my age and the already progressed state of my disease. He also told me that he wished he would have met me two years earlier. This was hard to hear. I mean, it validated all of my concerns and the struggle I had been in for those two years, but I wondered where I would be had someone, anyone, taken me seriously. He also mentioned the possible need "down the road" for a transplant, but his hope was that with aggressive drug therapy we might be able to slow the progression of the disease and buy me some time, perhaps a few years. I would be placed on some prednisone (10mg) and mycophenolate (1000mg, twice a day), Bactrim (3X week), and he'd set me up for a Rituxan infusion for my RA. Before I left his office, I was given two pneumonia vaccines, as well as a tetanus booster. Once I started these medicines, particularly the mycophenolate (an immunosuppressant), vaccine efficacy would be suspect at best. Also, I was told to stop working part time. He also told me that I would need to turn down my spot in the radiography program. I would return to see him in November and we'd see where I was at that point. My life, at this point, essentially came to a halt.

Erin and I left the appointment and went to lunch at a pizza place next door to the clinic, where we discussed our impressions. It had been quite a month. In September alone I had gone from not really knowing anything about my condition to being scared shitless. I did feel a little upbeat at this point as I ate my mushroom and pepperoni pizza. Heck, I had just seen a specialist who told me that we were going to be aggressive in treating this condition with medicines. For her part, Erin was adamant that the medicines would work and that any discussion of transplant was premature at best. While I shared her hope, I was not as optimistic about the medicines. Sure, I wanted them to work. Sure, I wanted to put off any talk of transplant for as long as possible. However, there was something nagging in me, some kind of inner voice that made me to feel less confident than her.

I suppose it's different when it's happening to you. We talked to our families about what was going on; we told our closest friends about my issues and what the next steps would be. My parents were obviously concerned. Heck, everybody was concerned and wanted to offer their help and support, but at this point there was little to be done except wait and see. I'd have to start these medicines, be on them for a bit, and see what happens.

But here's how it was different for me—it was me. Everyone else was able to move on with life, but I now felt like I had this storm cloud over my head, with no idea if or when it would burst forth with a storm that I wasn't sure I was ready to face. It was comforting to know that I had a good support group with my parents and our friends, but what could any of them really do? At that point, I could still drive and go to my kids' events—not that there were many to go to. Emma took advantage of not having a senior marching band season to play soccer one more time. Rachel kept on playing soccer and I was able to attend those games. For that I am grateful. I had no way of knowing at the time that I might not ever see another game. I had no way of knowing that I was dying. That's probably best. What I did notice as I attended these games is that I was moving slower and getting more winded as I walked to the fields.

At least I was there. And it was fun. I was sad that Emma lost out on her senior season of marching band. She had worked hard to be captain of the color guard and would not get the chance to lead those kids on the field or for her senior flag solo. With the soccer, she knew it was her last go-around and she was able to enjoy it as such. We all did. When you know something is coming to an end, and is quite possibly the final chapter you'll write on a certain segment of your life, it becomes easier to soak it all in. Watching Emma play that fall, I took it all in: her intensity, her competitiveness, and her joy. She had come a long way from the days at the YMCA soccer fields. She was becoming quite the young woman. Both of my girls were growing into phenomenal ladies. My reliance on them over the next few months would be crucial.

As I was writing what could potentially be my own last chapter, I was grateful they were at home with me and that I could be part of their day. The four of us spent every day in the same house: them in their rooms doing school, Erin in our room working, and me downstairs. But we were together and that would matter. However, for all of the good of us being together, I was starting to become sort of a prisoner in my home. We couldn't go anywhere overnight due to my oxygen needs, and it was getting more and more difficult for me to ambulate around as the fall progressed. October passed with little happening. I stopped working at my doctor's direction, the soccer season concluded, and I suddenly had nothing going on in my life. It started to be a lonely time for me even though I was in a house full of people. It was a hard time for me, to be certain. Everyone else had their activities, but me? I had nothing. My work was gone. My freedoms vanishing. My life becoming … what? I didn't know, and that was the horrifying part. I don't want to assume that it was easy for Erin and the girls. But at least they had the distractions of work and school to occupy their days. Everything I was looking to do was suddenly evaporating and I didn't know how to get it back. I had no way of knowing it at the time, but things were soon to get far, far more challenging.

My appointment with the specialist in November was fairly unremark-able, which was good—I guess. My PFTs from the prior week showed little change in overall function, and my saturation levels were a little lower, at 92%, but not low enough to qualify me for supplemental oxygen full time. Of note from a review of the specialist's notes on MyChart, though, is that according to him I was approaching my window for transplant. He did say that we were still a bit early with the medicines to see if they were working. I was having doubts. My overnight oxygen levels were increased to 4 liters and I got the feeling he was not happy with where things were heading. So I guess calling this an unremarkable visit is wrong. It was remarkable in that I was showing more and more desaturation, greater O2 needs, and he was increasing some medicine dosages. My blood pressure was through the roof and my heart rate was in the 120s. These are not normal, but at this point it was what was starting to pass for an unremarkable visit to a doctor. He also looked like he was starting to take my deteriorating situation personally. I can't really speak for how he felt, so maybe I'm projecting my feelings on him. That's just my impression. It's like he felt like he had thrown the heavy-hitters at me and it was having little to no effect. I just felt worse. While some of my diagnostics were more or less fine, he noticed that everything I did was more labored than before. My next appointment with him would be in six to eight weeks. I'd see the folks at Rex in about a week or so.

My birthday came and went, and despite the efforts of my family, I didn't feel much like celebrating. It just felt like I was recognizing a date that might not come around again. It was hard to celebrate the passing of another year when the next one felt so uncertain. Thanksgiving was a muted affair as well. I was simply in no mood to be thankful for anything, and I was struggling to find happiness in my life. While I was certainly blessed to have such a wonderful family and support group, I was in the doldrums. My physical status had gotten so bad that I wasn't even able to walk around the Christmas tree lot with the family.

To me it felt like I was on an inexorable march to a worse-case scenario. I was treading a path toward transplant. It was not a path I wanted, and not one I was sure I could handle. For Erin's part, she kept her head down and focused on the here and now. She tried to remain positive for me. And again, I can't speak for her, but I think even she was getting nervous. By the time we reached the end of November, I was starting to have more and more trouble just functioning, and it was noticeable to everyone. For the first time in our marriage and as a dad, I couldn't help with decorating for Christmas. I just sat there and watched. I could no longer help out in the kitchen. Doing any kind of chore was starting to be impossible. I didn't help with leaves this fall. All in all, as November progressed I became more and more useless. I was proud of the girls for how they were stepping up, but I felt I didn't have any purpose or point. Any kind of intimacy with Erin was gone. I just didn't have it in me any more to do anything. I was truly reaching a low point in my life. I have struggled with depression type concerns before, but this was next level. My role as a father was diminishing, my role as a provider was gone, my role as helper at home was gone, my role as a husband had disappeared. All I was was a roommate, and an absolutely useless one. Things were bad for me. But they were about to get worse.

December 2020

December 6 would be the last day I left the house for anything other than a doctor's visit. A friend had rented out a theater and we, along with three other families, went to see National Lampoon's Christmas Vacation. It was fun, but not without struggle. Erin parked in the spot closest to the door, but I still had to sit down before making it inside. Some of the kids who went with us were shaken by seeing me so sick. Once in the theater, I didn't really want to move. It was nice doing an activity. But it was my last, as it happened.

December 7 would prove to be my own "day of infamy," when everything started to change in a hurry. December 7 was the last day I would drive. I shouldn't have, but Erin had to work and I thought I could get myself to my appointment at Rex. Even though I parked near the doors, I had to sit on the bench outside the entry for a minute or two. Then, when I got to the elevator, I had to lean against the wall, huffing and puffing the whole time. One thing that people who are struggling to breathe love is when people offer suggestions on how to catch your breath. Lady—I can't freaking breathe, and I can't take a deep breath. At this point I'm probably in the 30s for lung function, so back off. Explaining this to you is taking more effort than I have. A simple nod in my direction acknowledging my struggle would more than suffice. Sometimes, that is all we need—to be seen.

The doctor was surprised to see me there alone. It was the only time in this entire process that Erin wasn't with me. I'm not sure what she could have done. But I was alone. The doctor came in and took a gander at me. I must've looked like hell. I know that everything was labored for me at this point. My blood pressure was OK (by my standards), my heart rate was still elevated, and my initial blood saturation was 86%. Now we're starting to get somewhere. I knew that for insurance to approve supplemental oxygen, I had to be below 90%. He wanted me to do another six-minute walk. I have never been able to figure out why six minutes is some magical number, but I'd only have to do it two more times as fate would have it. The nurse put the cannula on me, and off we went. I desaturated quickly and stayed low. Even when she turned on the oxygen, I stayed below 90. While a bit disconcerting, it was great news. I thought I'd be able to get oxygen approved and maybe gain some type of mobility again when I was at home. I figured wrong. It helped initially to get the supplemental oxygen, but I was getting so sick, so fast, that it would soon get to the point where the oxygen just couldn't keep up.

All of this bothered the doctor. It was enough of a concern that before the day was out, I had talked to him again by phone, as well as the specialist over in Chapel Hill. My condition was rapidly worsening. Based on the impression of the doctor at Rex and some of my numbers, the specialist told me that he was referring me to the transplant team for evaluation. I'm glad that I was at home for this call. I'm glad Erin was with me for this. I'm not sure I could've made it home if I had gotten this news in the doctor's office. It was a bombshell. In little over three months, I had gone from having no clue what was wrong with me, to getting a diagnosis, to being referred to the transplant team.

As it would turn out, this would be the last time I saw the pulmonologist at Rex. My disease would require more immediate attention now, so much so that by the time December 7 came to a close, I had an appointment to get an echocardiogram to make sure my heart was strong enough to move forward with the transplant evaluation process, and I'd be on oxygen around the clock. I was now tethered to a compressor all the time. I could travel at most 50 feet—either that or learn how to budget oxygen canisters and calculate airflow and how long I'd be gone. We'd get good at that. I was also told to increase my airflow to 8/10 liters of oxygen. My needs would soon increase.

On December 10 we traveled to Meadowmont in Chapel Hill for the echo. That was a non-event, except that it was the first time we budgeted oxygen needs. I learned that a key question I would need to ask was, "Do you have oxygen available?" You would think that it would be a given that a clinic or a hospital would. You would be wrong. I've said that part of this process is learning to advocate for yourself. Another big part is learning how to play the game. Asking these questions, budgeting oxygen needs, being sick (but not too sick)—all of this is gamesmanship. We would get tired playing the game, but we couldn't skip a turn. I was in it for keeps. But there are some things you just can't fake. I can give great answers, I can ask good questions, I can do all of those things. I can't fake diagnostics. I would have to trust my body to not lie, and thankfully the echo revealed that my heart was strong enough to move forward. I was heading to transplant for evaluation.

How does one celebrate the holidays with this lingering over their head? Poorly, in my case. I was not in any kind of a festive mood. Everything we normally did was shot all to hell. Family events didn't happen, not really. I was tethered, remember? I couldn't really get around the house. Once I came downstairs in the morning, I stayed. Going back up required me to rest at the halfway point. Man, I'd even desaturate getting up to go to the bathroom in the middle of the night. The lowest number I ever saw was 59%. That's low, friends. I wasn't able to go shopping like normal so I did a fair amount of online shopping. I was trying to take some weight off of Erin, since I wasn't really useful around the house. My feelings of uselessness were only getting worse. I had no appetite, no joy in anything. Normally on Christmas Eve, the four of us would get fancy and go out to eat. Once back home, Erin and I would open a great bottle of wine, watch *Love Actually*, and once that was over set up the "Santa" gifts for the girls. There would be no fancy dinner this year. The bottle of wine had no taste for me, and I only made it through about 45 minutes of the movie before I was wiped out. Erin went upstairs to get the presents. Not just the girls', but also the stuff I had bought for her. Dammit. I couldn't even set out presents for my wife and kids. What the hell use was I? To say that Erin was picking up my slack is an understatement. The girls were too.

My parents came up as normal on Christmas, but for me it wasn't much fun. Everything required effort—everything. I had gotten so much worse, so quickly, it was getting hard to even comprehend. It sapped all of the joy from the season, adding yet one more loss to the ledger that was this year. Erin's parents and uncle came by later in the day to bring me my gifts. Her family gathered later in the week to celebrate, but given my oxygen, I'd be staying at home. Not to say that her family didn't make an effort to come and visit me. Her brother and sister made lots of effort to keep their family healthy enough to come and see me. I'm not sure they exactly bargained for what they saw. I appreciated their efforts and their company, even if I was less than vibrant. I'm happy that her family had a good time and I'm glad they were able to have some type of normal activity in an abnormal year. But I was alone.

New Year's Eve was just as joyless for me. There was no need to celebrate 2021 at this point, because everything was up in the air. The only certainty was that I was dying. Looking back on it, there's no other way to describe it. I was dying, and all I could do was focus on the daily. I used to ride motorcycles. One time I was riding in the mountains on a particularly curvy stretch of road. I found that if I looked too far ahead of myself, I'd get too loose in the current curve and potentially lose control. The only curve that mattered was the one I was in. Navigate that one safely and then move to the next one. After you navigated them all, you'd reach the end in one piece. That would be how the next few months would play out. I'd need to navigate each curve as it came, I just had no idea as the new year began how many curves I'd face. If I looked too far ahead, I was destined to crash. I had to focus on the now. If I did that, maybe—*maybe*—I'd reach the end of this road in one piece. To be honest, the now was all I had. The way I was feeling, I wasn't sure what was left. I was glad to be done with 2020. I know we all were.

I need to hit a pause button before we move on to January of 2021. 2020 was an absolute crap year and there is no way to argue against that. There will be volumes written about the year: the pandemic, the Black Lives Matter movement, the election, and everything else that went down. In our house, things were no less significant, though no one, other than me, will ever record what happened. I've hit on a few things so far. The year started with such promise. Rachel, as noted, completed her basketball season and was made captain of the school soccer team. She played one game before the season was shut down. I wasn't there as I was tending to Emma and her broken down car at the Sheetz. Rachel lost out on all of the end-of-school celebrations at Magellan. She had been there, with the same kids, since third grade. When I chaperoned her trip to Greensboro on February 7, we had no way of knowing that it would be the last field trip she would ever have.

Emma's winter guard season never even happened. She had some rehearsals, and they did the parent preview, so I got to see her perform, but that was it. This was becoming a theme that would carry not only through this year, but even into 2021: the suddenness with which things were changing. It was almost as if every minute something was happening, and it was all outside of our control. By the middle of March, the girls were done on campus. Rachel's "graduation" happened online, Emma's band banquet was online, basically our lives moved online. 2020 was going to be a great year for me attending concerts. In February, Erin and I were able to slip away for a weekend to Beaufort. At the end of that weekend, Erin came down with a mysterious lung issue (yeah, it was COVID). She managed to rally, and two weeks later we attended our last in person concert for the foreseeable future, Tim Barry at the Cat's Cradle in Carrboro. and as good as it was, it wasn't the last concert I was hoping for. I had tickets to see Against Me! at Motorco in Durham. That was the first casualty. In quick succession, I lost Josh Ritter at The Haw River Ballroom, and then Jason Isbell at the Durham Performing Arts Center. That was just through June. Things were shutting down all over the world and we were losing control of our lives. We did manage to get

Erin's three-season room built right at the beginning of the pandemic, and it's where we would spend most of the rest of the year.

Musicians like Frank Turner and Josh Ritter launched weekly online shows as fundraisers for small venues and charities. These became a staple for me. Cory Branan did a few as well and I loved them too. Music and books became a great sustainer for me through the year. I read, listened to music, and continued my guitar lessons. Once the summer was over and school resumed online, it was getting harder for me to enjoy things. The pandemic had begun to drag on and I was having more and more trouble keeping the girls motivated. They were champs and did everything expected and asked of them, but you could tell they were growing weary. We all were. As fall progressed and my condition worsened, so did my ability to even enjoy music and books. Playing guitar became difficult, and it got to the point where about the only time I'd pick it up was when my lesson occurred. One can't improve that way, but it was just exhausting to do much of anything other than sit. I mentioned how crappy the holidays were, and they were indeed unpleasant, but I will give Rachel credit for getting me a gift that really did inspire me and give me some hope. On her own, she contacted Frank Turner in England and got him to record a message for me. It was meant to hopefully give me some inspiration as we moved into a new year. As it turns out, as we began 2021, I'd need all kinds of hope.

2021

January

As January 2021 started the girls were still attending school online as they closed out their fall semesters, which they did with tremendous success. Rachel achieved straight As and Emma only had one B, and that was in an AP class. All in all, good work. We had been hoping that once the spring semester started, they would be back on campus in some form, but that too was changing on a minute-to-minute basis. Eventually, it was decided they would remain online. As disappointing as that was for them, for me it was a ray of light. At this point, I was pretty much useless. I couldn't even get up to get drinks or food. The only thing I was able to do on my own was go to the bathroom. Our family and friends would be shocked and concerned when they would stop by for a visit. I was spending my days alone as everyone else was occupied, and by the time they were done, I had no energy left. I'd usually struggle through dinner, half eating whatever was served, and then hobble upstairs. All this while chained to the oxygen compressor. Everything in my life had become nearly impossible. Activities that used to take minutes were taking much longer; activities that weren't essential were scrapped. I have cut my own hair for years. It's usually a fairly insignificant event requiring little effort or time. Now, it was just downright hard. Erin would set up a chair for me, clippers at the ready, and I'd fight to get to the chair and shave my head while seated. I'd have to pause to move the oxygen line out of the way on each side and then keep going. I suppose it didn't matter how bad it looked. I wasn't going anywhere or seeing anyone anyway.

After cutting my hair, I'd work my way to the shower, where Erin had set up the shower chair and gotten the water to the right temperature. I'd sit there and try to bathe myself as best as I could. It got to the point where showering every day became too much of an issue. I could only muster enough energy every other day or so. On days when I couldn't get to the shower, Erin would bring me a washcloth and I'd do my best to clean off. She became adamant that I at least wash off, put on fresh deodorant, and change clothes. I was turning into an absolute slob, but I really just didn't give a damn. Even on days when I showered and felt as fresh as possible, the very effort of showering was almost more than I could take. After getting dressed, I'd fall back in bed almost immediately, and it would take some time before I was recovered enough to even try and catch a TV show.

I was becoming a drain on everyone in the house. I was glad to have company at home though. The girls would come in to my room or down-stairs to see me between classes and give me life updates. They were also bringing me drinks and food. Without them, I'd have starved. Even as it was I was beginning to waste away. Erin, for her part, was logging thousands of steps just going back and forth, getting me things I might need. Only with the benefit of hindsight do I now realize just how absolutely useless I was, and what a drain on the entire family I was. I can't even begin to know how stressful it was for them and I still don't know how they kept it together. I guess my girls are strong. We were all just trying to ride the current curve; we couldn't even look down the road. Any attempts to make plans were futile. By January, many of our friends and family were getting vaccines and starting to make plans for trips or small outings. But we were still stuck. My oxygen chain saw to that.

For now we were operating day to day. I had been referred to the transplant team, been contacted by the financial representative, and been called by the scheduler. All we could do was wait for January 12 for my first round of pre-transplant evaluations to begin. Before those appointments began, I had one more visit with the PA at Rex. When I saw her on January

7, my condition was so bad, I'm fairly certain she was in tears. My vital signs were crap: my blood pressure was elevated, my pulse at rest was 133 BPM, and my oxygen saturation was 93%—and that was on 10L of oxygen now. The specialist had increased my levels again. I had also lost 12 pounds, bringing me down to 171. I left that appointment with no real changes and not knowing if I'd ever have the chance to speak with her again.

The specialist had mentioned my "window for transplant" back in December. I was in it for sure. That meant that I was sick enough to need transplant but not so sick that my outcome wouldn't be positive. It meant that my weight was within a certain range—not too heavy, not too light. It meant that my strength was still decent: I was in pretty good shape before, and I got so sick, so fast that I retained some residual strength. Basically, being in "my window" meant that I was Goldilocks. Not too much of any one thing, just right. There would be some tests that I would need to pass, others that I would need to fail (for lack of a better word), and others I'd just have to endure. I was sick enough that, had these been normal times, I would have been admitted to the hospital and all of my pre-transplant testing would have been completed over the course of a few days. As it stood, the COVID numbers in early to mid-January were spiking in North Carolina, so I'd be doing everything over the course of a week or so.

The process, for me, went like this:

1. Referral

2. Insurance Approval

3. Scheduling of tests/appointments

4. Testing and appointments

5. Team meets to decide if I am a candidate

6. Back to Insurance for transplant approval

7. Listing on the transplant database

8. Wait

9. Wait some more

10. IF a match is found—new lungs

This is a wild oversimplification of what I was about to endure, as you'll see.

January 12

January 12 would go down as one of the worst days of this journey. Because of the advanced stage of my disease and how sick I was, it was imperative that I progress as quickly as possible through all of the testing. It would be an endurance test, and one that, if I didn't pass, would have deadly consequences. Heck, I've been sick before. Never in my life did I feel as terminal as I did on that day. It would get worse. The night before my appointment, Erin and I had done the math to figure out exactly how much oxygen we'd need to pack in the car and take with us to make sure I could breathe throughout the day. It was a pretty good amount, and it made me feel like I was riding in a bomb. By this point I was on a flow of around 12 liters, meaning the large bottles of oxygen would last around an hour. Between drive times, getting from the car, to the check-in, to the designated location, to everywhere else I'd need to go … Well, it was a lot. We used the valet service at the hospital and got very efficient at that step. We'd stop, unload, get out just enough oxygen to get back to the car in a few hours, and head inside.

On the twelfth I had several appointments. Again, it's important to remember that these appointments are usually spread over weeks. Today I would have blood drawn, imaging done, a PFT, and then I'd meet the other pulmonary specialist. All beginning at 7:30am. We hopped in the line to get in the hospital, answered their COVID questions, and went to check-in. My blood draw was quite the event. They would need to draw so much blood, the phlebotomist would have to switch arms and re-tap. By the time she was done, she had taken around 25 vials of blood from my arms. It was so much blood I expected cookies and a coke at the end. What's more, there was no oxygen available in the phlebotomy lab, so I was hooked up to my tank. For what wouldn't be the last time, we kept a nervous eye on the regulator to see how much air I had left.

After this step, we rounded the corner to take the elevators to the basement of the Women's Hospital to the radiography lab. All of these locations would become very familiar to me over the next few months, but the first time is always special. It's kind of like the first time you go to a new restaurant, ya know? What's the procedure? How do I order? What's the best thing to get here? What I would learn is that the bracelet I received at check-in was a sort of "fast pass" that allowed me to skip the line waiting to use the kiosk used to check in other folks. It made me special. That and the wheelchair and the oxygen and the dying. The radiography waiting room also resembled the waiting room at the DMV. There were all manner of folks in there with varying degrees of the skills needed to navigate the medical care jungle. And just like in the jungle, or the DMV, we would see our fair share of arguments and near-fights. This waiting room was a special place to spend a few minutes. Eventually, I was called, and Erin wheeled me into the X-Ray room. I struggled to my feet and had my imaging done. First, I faced the radiographic cassette.

"Take a deep breath and hold it" the radiologist said.

"A deep breath? Are you kidding? Do you know why I'm here?" I replied.

I inhaled as deeply as I could, which wasn't much, and she got the image. I turned to my right and grabbed the bar above my head and she snapped a side-view. I was spent and collapsed back in my wheelchair. At least I was on their oxygen, as this room had an O2 port. It seemed like my time in radiography had lasted hours. I had expended so much energy doing what they needed me to do. It had, in fact, been about five minutes.

The results of the imaging were as expected:

"Reticular opacities throughout bilateral lung fields consistent with known interstitial lung disease and severe fibrosis." Something weird, though, is that even though I had had imaging done prior to this visit, the imaging used to compare x-rays was from December 2010. Unsurprising to no one was that "There is volume loss compared to the relatively distant prior exam."

With two of my appointments down and three more to go, we were on our way.

This was Erin's first time trying to drive a wheelchair, and though she would get really good at it, today was not her day. There were lots of collisions with door frames, elevator doors, really anything. She never hit any people, so that was a win, and I managed to not get dumped on the floor. It must've been exhausting and I'm not sure I fully understood just how hard she was working to keep me going and to get me from Point A to Point B. Not only was she pushing me and my oxygen, but she was carrying a book bag laden with all sorts of paperwork, drinks, and snacks. She had to have resembled a pack mule. I'm sure we made for quite a sight as we moved about the hospital. From radiography in the basement of the Women's Hospital we had to go to the sixth floor of the main hospital, to the Pulmonary Function Lab. This visit was awful. Here I would do the test again to measure my FEV1 and FVC again, but I'd also have to do the six-minute walk. I didn't realize it at the time, but this 6 minute walk was the most important six minutes of my life.

The results of my flow testing were also exactly what we thought. By now, I had lost even more function. I was down to an FVC 1.36L (31%); FEV1 0.91L (25%). My lungs were shit and getting worse by the day. It'd be untruthful to say I didn't feel validated in all of my previous concerns, but at this point I didn't care about validation. I just wanted to live. I guess you could consider this a "failed test," but that was OK. This was one of those tests that a failure on was a good thing. It showed that my lung efficiency and capacity was no longer really able to support my continued … What's the word? Life. That's the word.

For my six-minute walk I had to walk 1,000 feet in six minutes. Before I began the walk I learned that if I was unsuccessful in reaching the 1,000 feet, that would mean a delay in the process. I would have to go to pulmonary rehab and gain some strength to qualify for transplant. This was all part of that window I found myself in, and because of that, this walk took on new meaning. All of the stubbornness and competitiveness, all of the traits I have always had, that were sometimes detrimental to me, became my biggest asset. When the pulmonary function technician explained the importance of this test, my entire demeanor changed. Usually this is the absolute last test done in the process, or so I was told. For me, because of how sick I was, it was happening at the beginning. Apparently, you're supposed to be evaluated by pulmonary therapy first of all, to see if you're strong enough for the process. In my case, there was no time for this ticky-tack crap. I was moving quickly through the transplant process. My window might be closing.

One good thing about this test was that I would be allowed to use as much oxygen as I'd need to stay adequately perfused. I just had to complete the walk. The technician hooked me up to a non-rebreather mask and a nasal cannula and cranked the oxygen. I was now getting 27 liters of oxygen. This is an insane amount of pure O2 and even on this much air I was still desaturating. But, here I go—walk. Walk to that cone, loop around it, and come back. Repeat. Then repeat some more. I was moving as fast as my little legs and failing body would go, and by golly, I did it. I exceeded the requirement, completing 315 meters or 1,033 feet. I was good to go. I was exhausted. I was wiped completely out and needed to sit. It would take my poor body quite some time to return to whatever was passing for normal these days. This was a small but important victory on my path. Without successfully completing this walk, I'm not sure how things would have panned out. I'm also not sure I had another 1,000 feet in me. It was, by far, the farthest I had walked in months. I was done walking for now as Erin wheeled me to the elevator and down to the fourth floor to the Transplant Clinic.

After checking in at the clinic and waiting just a moment or two, I was called back. My vital signs were pretty much in line with what they had been. My blood pressure was slightly elevated, though of little concern. My heart rate was bopping along at 124 beats per minute. My weight was down to 171 pounds. No matter what I did, I couldn't get my heart to slow down. No amount of oxygen or rest would cause the rate to drop. Turns out, there was a reason for this. My heart was having to work extra hard to move really crappy blood through my body. Not only was the oxygen level a concern, but I also had a good amount of carbon dioxide in my system. My heart was doing work it didn't need to be doing. The doctor came into the room and we started the evaluation.

It's an interesting phenomenon in a lung transplant how little "evaluating" is done in the office. They would listen to my lungs, note bilateral crackles that were consistent with the diagnosis, and listen to my heart. They'd look at my ankles to check for swelling. The large majority of the diagnostic work seemed to come from lab results and imaging. I suppose it makes sense with the benefit of hindsight. Heck, he can't exactly look at my lungs from the outside. I just never really pieced together how crucial the imaging and lab work and PFTs would be. This is where the game comes in. I couldn't control any of that. The only thing I could control was my effort on the walk (again, amazing) and how well I presented myself to the doctor. It felt like a job interview and I was just answering questions. Reading back through his notes though, apparently I did a good job presenting myself. Erin and I received good reviews. We were knowledgeable and engaged with a good understanding of my medical condition and therefore "based on my evaluation appears to be a good candidate."

By now we were done at the hospital and it was time to make our way back to the car. It's a good thing, too, as I was starting to get very low on my oxygen, and we needed to get back to our stockpile in the car. After four appointments before noon, most people would call it a day and go home to get some rest. Not us. No way, no how. We still had one more appointment to go. There are things that are getting harder to remember as time progresses. Between the passing of time and my decreased brain function, I can't for the life of me remember if Erin and I went to lunch or not that day. For some reason, I seem to remember that I wasn't supposed to eat anything prior to my last appointment. As I have come to be reminded many times, I remember things that didn't happen and can't remember things that did, so who really knows? Whether I ate or not, I guarantee that we made sure that Erin got something. Erin was and is a true badass. She was working her ever-loving tail off getting me around, and this was only the first day.

My appointment for the CT scan, without contrast, was not at the hospital. Fortunately it was on our way home from town. Unfortunately, this was the only appointment that was running behind and made me wait. Even the little old lady doing the COVID screening was a pain. I had to struggle to get in the door as there was no wheelchair, and she wanted to start peppering me with questions right away. It was all I could do to answer them, and then she wanted to offer advice on how to breathe. I was probably shorter with her than she deserved and I am sorry for that, but be damned, it had already been a day. I checked in, sat down, and waited. I waited so long that Erin came inside and started to regulate my oxygen. I was getting down to the wire on the air in my tank and needed to get hooked up to wall oxygen. It's a weird thing: when you see the regulator trending down, you start to regulate your breathing so you don't run out of air. It's counter-intuitive to what you should do, I guess. Once I got back to the room where the imaging was done and was able to do so, I could breathe a bit more freely. I lay down on the table, and the non-contrast, high-resolution CT chest was performed with inspiratory (breathe in), expiratory (breathe out), and prone series. Guess what? I was sick. The CT scan showed what the x-rays did, just a more clear picture of it. The exact findings were:

"Clear central tracheobronchial tree. Diffuse bronchial wall thickening, traction bronchiectasis, reticular opacities and architectural distortion which is slightly more predominant at the lung apices. There is minimal honeycombing in the superior segment of bilateral lower lobes. No definitive air trapping on expiratory views. No pleural effusion" and

"Extensive pulmonary fibrosis consistent with rheumatoid arthritis associated interstitial lung disease."

So yeah, I was sick, and now it was on imaging for all the world to see. We were now approaching five p.m. and we had been in Chapel Hill all freaking day. It had been a hard one for us both. I'd been poked, tested, questioned, and imaged. Erin had gotten me everywhere I needed to be and was, not for the last time, a rock. A definite theme was emerging. There is no way I would have been able to do this without her. Home we went. Exhausted, she got us home. All we wanted to do was get me upstairs to bed and get both of us some rest. We were emotionally and physically spent. The news was mixed. I was on my way toward a potential transplant, but for now I was still sick and getting worse by the day. Our spirits were in a delicate place when Emma came to our door.

"Guys," she said. "I have COVID."

This pronouncement sent Erin over the edge. She cried. The biggest thing that could derail all of this would be for me to get COVID. I could pass all of the testing, be listed, and get the call. Upon arrival at the hospital, I'd be tested for COVID, and a positive test would end my chance at those lungs. This was devastating news for all of us. Emma was bummed that she got COVID, but the impact it would have on all of us was huge. That night was the last time I saw Emma for the next 10 days as she exiled herself to her room to quarantine. Rachel, too, would be "quarantined" from school through Emma's 10 days and an additional 14 after that. In the house, Erin and Rachel wore a mask every time they came near me. I never left my room. At meal times we all ate in different rooms and FaceTimed each other on our phones. Erin and Rachel would tested negative for COVID repeatedly over the next few days. But the absolute strain it placed on what was already a difficult situation was hard to put into words.

Fortunately, Emma had a very mild case and recovered quickly, and no one else got sick. There would be harder, more challenging days ahead for sure. As we look back, though, January 12 is one of those days that really jump out. Maybe it's because it was the first real day of testing and trying to get listed for transplant. I don't know. On its own, the day of appointments in Chapel Hill would've been enough. Emma getting COVID would have been enough on its own, too. It was just starting to feel like the universe was just piling on. Having these two significant things occur on the same day just went to show the absolute unpredictability of life. There is no reason things happen. They just do. This was one more thing we had to deal with. One more curve to navigate and come out the other side. One more test in a year of exams.

January 13

I'm not sure which day was harder on us, January 12 or 13. January 12 required us to drive to Chapel Hill and me to go through some initial testing while Erin had to do her own kind of heavy lifting. January 13 we were able to stay home and do three separate consultations. It was nice to stay home and not make the drive, but being interviewed by doctors of three separate disciplines was exhausting. By this point, any basic conversation was essentially non-existent. I could talk, sure, but my speech was halting and labored. I was having to carefully measure how much and how frequently I spoke. I had no real volume, and trying to carry on these chats was challenging at best. More than the appointments I had on the twelfth, these virtual appointments felt like interviews. On the twelfth the vast majority of what I did, or had done to me, was out of my hands. I couldn't control the lab results, the imaging, or PFTs. All I could do was hope that the results of those tests pointed in the right direction. Today, though, I would have to talk to a social worker, nutritionist, and psychologist.

First up was the social worker. Over the course of our talk I was asked questions like:

What kind of support did I have at home?

How was my insurance/ability to afford the procedure and after-care?

Would I need to relocate?

Looking back on it, I think that the outcome of this conversation would have the most direct impact on my acceptance. And looking back on it, that is scary. The whole time, it felt as if a wrong answer or bad impression was going to derail me and doom me. I was honest with everyone, but I was admittedly more guarded than usual. The truth is, I had a fantastic support network. From Erin, Emma, and Rachel, to our families, to our network of friends, I would have all the support I would need to get to appointments and function up to and after a transplant.

As for the insurance, we had had a conversation with a friend of ours who worked in the insurance business. We had expressed our issues with our coverage the previous year, and he'd put us in touch with an agent in town who could help us. With his help we were able to secure phenomenal insurance. We were paying pretty high premiums, but had a fairly low deductible and out of pocket maximum. And since premiums are tax deductible, it was OK. Erin had done all of the legwork on this piece of the puzzle and it was huge. The timing of all of this seemed to be working out pretty well, given the insurance had only taken effect at the beginning of the year.

The relocation factor, on the other hand, was one that neither of us had considered. It was news to us that we might need to be located within a certain distance of the hospital. Many folks needed to move to the Chapel Hill area for the duration of their testing, listing, and after-care. As difficult as heading back and forth to Chapel Hill would be, at least we'd be able to return home each day and sleep in our beds given our close proximity to Chapel Hill. Sort of. Because of Emma's COVID issues, Erin had moved into the bonus room and was now sleeping and living in there. Our last night sharing a bed ended up being January 11.

After convincing the social worker of what wonderful people we were—which was no lie—we had a short break before meeting with the nutritionist. It turned out that eating would prove to be one of the hardest pieces of this puzzle. It was also one of the parts that had Erin the most concerned. She worried about my ability to eat once in the hospital. My celiac is such that I am fairly sensitive to cross-contamination concerns, and the effects of a gluten incident are rough. Eight hours after getting glutened, my stomach will distend, and if it's a bad enough glutening it'll lead to gastric issues on both ends of my digestive tract. The most concerning end would be vomiting. Before transplant, it wouldn't be a real concern, but after—ho boy. Vomiting after getting new lungs could be life-threatening. There would be questions: Is the vomiting due to gluten issues? Medicines? Something else? We would have to be sure that we completely removed the gluten part of the equation from this problem. However, there is a bright side to having a food issue. After eight years of not being able to eat certain foods, removing others from my diet, as would be required post-transplant, would not be a problem. Apparently for some folks, this can be a deal breaker. It blows my mind that someone would rather eat at a buffet than get new lungs, but to each their own, I guess.

On this initial call the nutritionist went over my current diet and made sure that I was more or less eating healthy, and my weight and stuff were OK. To ensure I remained in this "window," I couldn't be too heavy or too light. The nutritionist had to put some people on special diets to either lose weight or bulk up. As for me, I was right where I should be.

But.

But I was losing weight at a rate that was starting to become concerning. Food just didn't taste good anymore and the effort required to eat had become a challenge. We decided that it would be important for me to switch to a protein shake like Ensure to make certain that my body didn't lose too much mass. So, as of January 13, I would have a chocolate milkshake with an Ensure in it almost every night. There would be a couple of blips of me having other things to eat, but it was always a chocolate shake. The nutritionist was less concerned over what I was going to eat for the near future. She was more concerned that I just get calories in me. I didn't think I was burning all that many calories since I was more or less confined to bed, but it turns out my body was working its skinny little ass off just trying to keep me alive. I had to have been a sight when people would see me. My clothes just hung off me and I was always cold. Nothing fit anymore. I suppose that describes more than just my clothes. Satisfied that she had pointed us in the proper direction, and with a follow-up the next week, we ended the day's second call.

By the time we spoke to the psychologist, I was done. I had no more energy or desire to talk with anyone. I would need to convince this lady that I wasn't crazy, wasn't in an abusive situation, and had the mental faculties to see this through. To this end, I was successful. I don't remember much about the conversation. Once she found out that I had been working with a therapist for years, she seemed happy. She also garnered that I had developed healthy coping skills and strategies. I guess all of my struggles to this point had been preparing me for this fight. After almost five hours of continuous conversations, we were done. I feel like I was more tired than ever. At least I was in bed.

In what would become a routine occurrence, I hit a new low. I thought I had been at the floor, but then I would move even farther down. There seemed to be no bottom to my fall, and I was down. I was getting sicker by the day. I was just trying to get on some magical list in the hopes that I would get lungs, and with each passing day, I felt like my life was slipping away. Emma was still quarantined in her room and would be through the twenty-second. Rachel would mask up to bring me drinks and food. She'd also come in to update me on her school days. Erin would stop by periodically to check on me and talk about her day. Those were the highlights. But I was alone. This was a lonely process, even lonelier in my case. Because of the COVID issues at home and people not wanting to jeopardize me, I had no real visitors for a while. I spent my days in my bed, reading, watching tv, listening to music, and trying not to die. I know that there was plenty of concern for me. It was hard on my wife and children watching me waste away. It had to be hard on my parents watching me suffer. Our friends were concerned; it showed on their faces when I saw them. By the time January 13 wrapped up, I was questioning just how many days I had left. That's where I was. One of the items discussed by multiple providers were the risks associated with a transplant. The way I was looking at this, the risk to not move forward greatly outweighed any risk of transplant. If I got new lungs, I *might* die. If I didn't, I *would* die. That much was certain. It was starting to become a matter of time. Everyone seemed to sense this, but no one wanted to admit defeat. My battered body still had some fight left and I would need it. The following week was going to be another long one.

January 20

On the eighteenth I received a call from the nurse coordinator telling me that the team had met, and based on my testing and meetings the previous week, they were moving me forward in the process. There was lots of "hurry up and wait" throughout this whole journey. I was told that I'd be getting a call to set up the next round of testing. These tests were going to get a touch more invasive, but they were necessary to make sure that my body systems were healthy enough to have a transplant. I got the impression that nothing was a real deal-breaker, it just needed to be known and therefore managed. That was my impression, but I could've been wrong. It might have been that a bad result on a heart test or kidney test would end the journey. I guess I didn't really want to know the truth about this. I was still living in the land of hope. That was all I had at this point, hope that things would work out. Within 10 minutes of this call, the scheduler had called me to tell me that she had set up the rest of my appointments. Apparently she had been told to make it happen and to do so with great haste. All I could do now was wait for the first appointments on the twentieth.

While I waited, I set up a CaringBridge page. There were lots of folks who were interested or concerned about me and we wanted a way to communicate with many of them at once. We figured that once I got to the hospital, it might get overwhelming for Erin to be responding to a million text messages, emails, etc. Also, we could control the flow of information and how much we shared with people. There wouldn't be the issue of me telling my mom or dad something and then there being something lost in the dissemination of the information to other concerned people. Not that anyone would deliberately mess up, but the amount of information to share was about to be monumental. I was a like a dam holding back a river of data. By setting up this page, I'd be able to let a little out at a time and not flood the folks downstream. It would also give me an outlet to the world.

On January 20 we drove to Chapel Hill for what was supposed to be two appointments. First up was a cardiac catheterization in the morning, followed by a visit to the pulmonary rehab folks in the afternoon. Well, that was the plan anyway. We had loaded the car up the night before with enough oxygen to summit Everest, packed a bag with a book or two (no food or water—dumb), and went to bed. I was nervous when we got up, but also a little excited. It felt like we were doing something. What, I didn't know, but something. So much of life is out of our hands. This was no different, but at least we were moving. We got to the hospital, and after deploying at valet, headed to check in.

"No, I've not been around anyone with COVID."

"No, I've not tested positive."

"No, I've not been out of the state."

"Well, yes, I do have a cough and shortness of breath, but they aren't COVID related."

To which the gatekeeper replies:

"Here's your mask. You may proceed."

Once arriving at check in:

"No, I've not been around anyone with COVID."

"No, I've not tested positive."

"No, I've not been out of the state."

"Well, yes, I do have a cough and shortness of breath, but they aren't COVID related."

To which the attendant then proceeds with the check-in process. I would be asked these same questions on every visit and on arrival at every clinic. I wondered how someone could get from the parking lot to the fourth or sixth floor with any kind of answer other than the ones I provided. Part of the game, I guess.

We made it to the cath lab, got checked in and prepped, and then were told to wait, because there were a few patients ahead of us in line. The good news: we had our own cubicle with our own TV and we were using hospital oxygen! My appointment was scheduled for nine a.m., and since I had my own cubicle with a TV, we watched some of the inauguration with our nurse. Clearly, I wouldn't be taken back on time, but at least the TV helped to pass the time. And being on hospital oxygen made it better, though any trip to the bathroom required me unhooking from the hospital oxygen and getting back on a tank. They finally took me back at eleven thirty. I hadn't yet eaten nor had anything to drink since seven a.m. as directed. Once I was wheeled into the procedure room I was greeted by my cath team. There were a couple of nurses, a doctor or two, maybe an anesthesiologist, and a large TV. They would use the TV to monitor the progress of the catheter into my body. The plan was to go in through the neck. That was the plan.

Things do not always go according to plan. Apparently, this would be a no-go, and they used what looked to be an ultrasound type device on my carotid vein. This would be the easiest and least invasive way to go in, but each time I exhaled, the vein would collapse. It would be impossible to go in this way. The other option was to go in my femoral vein. The decision was made and someone yanked, ever so gently, my underoos down to my ankles. It should be noted at this point, as I was sitting there in all my naked glory, that the doctor was young, female, and attractive. However, for the first time in this journey, but not the last, all modesty was gone. There I was, for all the world to see (or have a good chuckle). I decided that it would be better for them to laugh with me than at me, so I started cracking jokes. It was easy to be funny with your drawers around your ankles. It got easier when the nurse broke out the electric razor to shave my "thigh" area. The vibrations from the razor made me chuckle—it tickled. The jokes flowed.

"Please be careful with that razor down there," I said. "I need you focused. I'm only here for a catheterization not a castration."

Zingers like that flowed from me like wine from the carafe of Bacchus. Properly sterilized (against infection, not reproduction), shaved, and prepped—in through the groin they went. As this was happening in the procedure room, the nurse immediately told Erin that the recovery would be longer. She called our scheduler, who moved our afternoon appointment to another day. It was for the best. After what I was to endure, there was no way a rehab evaluation would be possible.

It's a weird feeling watching a cardiac catheterization. This long tube is inserted into you femoral vein, and you see it as it works its way like a worm from your leg into your abdomen, into your chest and your heart. You're watching this worm infiltrate the innermost parts of your body, and it's not normal. I didn't feel anything, at least I don't think I did. At one point, I thought I may have felt a little flutter when the catheter got to my heart, but I could've imagined that. The point of the entire procedure was to make sure pressures were good internally and that there was no reason my heart couldn't take the surgery and recovery. That was my perspective. According to the doctor's notes:

"Under Lidocaine 2% local anesthesia, a 7F sheath was placed in the right femoral vein using modified Seldinger technique. A balloon-tipped catheter was introduced into the sheath. The balloon was inflated, and the catheter was advanced through the right heart chambers into the pulmonary wedge position. Right-sided pressures were obtained, PA saturations were drawn, and thermodilution was performed in triplicate. Upon completion, the PA catheter was removed, and the sheath was removed. Manual pressure was applied until hemostasis was achieved."

That sounds fancy, huh? Once the doctor was done and the catheter was out, it was time for a return to my eight-by-eight cell for what would be a very long recovery time. Finally, I got to drink! And eat! I only had a few snacks in my bag, so Erin headed off to the cafe to grab some more things. The hospital didn't do gluten free well in the quick service setting, so I was destined to consume a Snickers and a bag of stale Doritos. And here was where the real fun began …

Upon arrival back to my luxurious recovery suite, I was told that I'd need to lie there, horizontal, for around 30 minutes. At that point, they would check to make sure that there were no hematoma developing. If all was clear, I'd be allowed to put my jeans back on and we could head on out. By the way, under no circumstances are blue jeans a good idea for attire when one has to have procedures performed at the hospital. Dress for comfort, folks, not style. It would be a two-hour total recovery time. If a hematoma developed, I'd have to start the clock all over again. Erin had gone to grab herself something to eat and while she was gone, sure enough, I developed a hematoma at the entry point which meant pressing down on the spot for 15 minutes and then starting the two-hour recovery over again.

A word about the pressing down on the spot process is needed. It was not gentle pressure. It was intense, hard, unrelenting pressure. The hematoma resembled an egg under my skin and the only way to treat it was to apply enough pressure to break it up and allow it to disperse under my skin. I would have a bruise, but it had to be done. The nurse called Erin and told her what was happening. In very, very short order Erin was back at the clinic and she looked a tad nervous. In a nutshell (ha), this is the scene and dialogue she encountered (as best as I remember):

Scene: A large, male nurse applying intense pressure to my nether regions. OK, my groin/thigh, but still. My underwear are around my waist at this point. The nurse and I are engaged in conversation.

"So … how 'bout them Tar Heels?" I say.

"Yeah, they seem to be coming around," he replies.

"Any thoughts on the NFL playoffs?" I ask.

"The Bucs look tough to beat, but the Packers might be a tough out," he answers.

And on like this it goes for around 20 minutes, as this large, friendly nurse applies intense pressure to my leg.

Now, we had to wait to see if another one developed or if I'd be clear to go. Two hours later, I got up, walked, got dressed, and thankfully went to the bathroom because, of course, I'd developed a second hematoma. Bam—back to another two hours of recovery. At this point, they were concerned enough that they paged the doctor who performed the procedure. Yeah, the young cute one. When she entered the suite, my pants and underwear were around my ankles. Here I am again for her to see in all my glory. It made me wonder if she requested this. Maybe I'm projecting. I don't know. She is not a large woman, so she really had to put her full weight into applying pressure. This act of mercy placed her very, very close to my … parts. I had to break the tension, because of course I did.

"You're going to have a very nasty bruise on your thigh and into your pelvic area for several days," she informed me.

"So, I should cancel my porn shoot for tomorrow?" I asked.

"I mean, it'd probably be best, though I'm sure there might be a market for this very specific type of porn," she replied.

I had found a kindred spirit. On like this we bantered for the time she had her face near my, you know. Every guy wishes for moments in life like this—well, not exactly like this, but I guess we make do. None of us are the Lotharios that we think we are. I had hoped that our paths would cross once again while I was going through my journey, but as fate would have it, I would never see her again. Once the second hematoma was dispersed into my leg and all of the doctors (because by now I was a medical side show for the cath lab) were convinced I was fine, I was allowed to pull my pants up and make ready to leave. Finally, I was informed that the results of my test were all good, so at least the pain was worth it. We had arrived at the hospital just before nine a.m. and didn't leave until six thirty p.m. I was supposed to have been done in enough time to make another appointment at two p.m. Thank goodness for Erin and the scheduler. At least we used hospital oxygen the whole time except for transport. Had I been forced to rely on oxygen tanks, who knows. It was a long, long, painful day. The procedure itself wasn't that bad. It was the recovery that just about whooped me. By the time I got home I was beyond exhausted, so straight to bed for me. I would have to return to the hospital the next day and be back there again at nine a.m.

January 21

And so we loaded the car up yet again with enough oxygen for a season of mountain climbing and returned to Chapel Hill. Hello again, valet people. Hello again, person asking questions about COVID:

"No, I've not been around anyone with COVID."

"No, I've not tested positive."

"No, I've not been out of the state."

"Well, yes, I do have a cough and shortness of breath, but they aren't COVID related."

To which the gatekeeper replies:

"Here's your mask. You may proceed."

Once arriving at check in:

"No, I've not been around anyone with COVID."

"No, I've not tested positive."

"No, I've not been out of the state."

"Well, yes, I do have a cough and shortness of breath, but they aren't COVID related."

Dammit, didn't I just answer these questions yesterday?? Well, yes, I had. But I would be answering them into perpetuity, it would seem.

Today I would be in the basement of the women's hospital for the majority of my appointments. I had a bone density scan to do, a barium swallow, another CT scan, and some type of imaging of my abdomen. Basically, they were checking my chest and abdomen to make sure everything in there was functioning as needed. These appointments were supposed to be spread out over the course of the entire day. Upon arriving in radiology I was called back to do my bone density scan 25 minutes early. Yep—early. The folks in radiology looked at all of my appointments and worked it out among themselves to do everything back to back. There was some waiting, but not too bad. I did the bone scan, a chest fluoroscope, at CT scan of my abdomen and pelvis, and then back to drink some barium to make sure my esophagus and all work right. I had an appointment for a blood draw at 11:30. I'll be darned, I made it. They compressed a full day into less than four hours, plus I could use their oxygen. After the mess that was the day before, today was mercifully short, and we were home by twelve thirty.

None of today's appointments were painful. Yay. First up was the bone density scan. I lay on a table and a machine whirred past my entire body, doing I don't know what. According to the notes:

"Dual energy x-ray absorptiometry was performed assessing the bone mineral density in the lumbar spine and proximal left femur using a Hologic Discovery W densitometer. The examination is compared with previous measurements dated 03/26/2012."

So, I guess that's what it did. The concern, in my understanding, is that over time bone density might decrease and lead to increased morbidity and mortality. Especially since one of the anti-rejection medicines could lead to an increase in osteoporosis. It was important that they establish where I was so they could monitor. Again, I'd learn that all of this, and all the data points moving forward, were baselines to learn to manage against. The results were as expected:

"Lumbar spine: Low bone density. The measurement has decreased significantly since prior study.

"Left proximal femur: Low bone density. The measurement has decreased significantly since prior study." I now had one more thing that we'd be monitoring.

Next up, a chest fluoroscopy. What is a chest fluoroscopy, you ask? According to John Hopkins:

"Chest fluoroscopy is an imaging test that uses x-rays to look at how well your lungs are working. It can also look at other parts of your respiratory tract. Your respiratory tract includes your lungs, nose, throat, trachea, and bronchi."

This test required the technician to obtain fluoroscopic spot images of the chest as I drew shallow breaths, deep breaths, and sniffs. And in what was becoming a pattern, the results were as expected and hoped for:

"Normal lung volumes. Pulmonary fibrosis. No focal airspace opacity, pleural effusion or pneumothorax. The cardiomediastinal silhouette is within normal limits. No acute osseous abnormality. There was normal excursion of the diaphragms with shallow breathing, deep breathing, and sniffing. No paradoxical motion identified."

All of this is to say that, other than the fact I was dying, my respiratory tract was working as it should. The only part of my respiratory tract that was deficient was my lungs. Admittedly, a crucial piece of the puzzle, but one we could fix. My nose, throat, trachea, and diaphragm were all working as expected. Hooray. On to the next test.

The next test was a CT scan of my abdomen, specifically the solid organs located therein, as well as my pelvic region. Mercifully, all I had to do was lay down again and let the machine do its magic. And by magic, I mean:

"A spiral CT scan of the abdomen and pelvis was obtained without IV contrast from the lung bases through the pubic symphysis. Images were reconstructed in the axial plane. Coronal and sagittal reformatted images were also provided for further evaluation."

To me it just seemed like magic. All of this would. My lower thorax was imaged, my spleen, pancreas, adrenal glands, kidneys, ureter, bladder, pelvic/ reproductive organs, GI tract, and I think that is all. And, just like every other test so far (for the most part) the results were unremarkable. Unremarkable is a good thing, as it turns out. All of my solid organs and everything else they imaged looked like it was supposed to look. Hooray again.

We're having so much fun, let's do one more procedure. A barium swallow! This test required me to drink barium and swallow. Shocking, right? It was done to make sure that when I swallowed, everything went in the right tube. Meaning, if I swallowed food or drink, it would end up in my stomach and not deviate into my lungs. Once I got my new lungs, I'd have to do this test again. We have to make sure nothing ends up in my lungs other than air. Barium is gross. It's a milky white substance with the viscosity of a thick yogurt drink, sort of like a smoothie, but gross. They gave me the option of combining it with either water or lemonade. Neither mattered. It was just nasty. Although in all honesty, as gross as the barium was, this was a pretty rad test to watch. On the screen beside where I stood, I was able to watch the workings of my upper GI tract do its thing. It was neat. I'd take a swig of the barium-infused water, hold it in my mouth, and when told to swallow, do just that. I could see the barium glowing white against the darkness of the image and follow it down from my mouth, down my esophagus, and out of sight. Once it had cleared any chance of going down my windpipe, the technicians were satisfied.

After the barium liquid, I also had to swallow a barium pill. This was to mimic food. I passed this without any difficulty. I won't put the entirety of the results down. It's enough to know that everything was normal. And just like that, we were done in radiology. All that was left was a quick stop at phlebotomy for another blood draw and we could go home. Today's blood draw was a small one. For today, they were concerned with my blood gas saturations/concentrations. And guess what? They were as expected. My venous carbon dioxide was high, and my venous oxygen was low. My O2 saturation was only 28%. Obviously the low O2 was a problem, as my body wasn't getting what it really needed, and the high CO2 was a concern too. High CO2 levels can lead to fatigue (check), headaches (check), shortness of breath (check), and high blood pressure (check). And there you have it. A day of testing that I passed. Everything was exactly as the doctors expected it to be in someone with ILD and RA. The very fact that everything was as good as it was was amazing.

It was nice to return home at a normal time, twelve thirty as opposed to the projected five thirty. I took advantage of the extra time and rested. My hip area was beginning to resemble modern art with the bruise I had developed. I named it "Hawaiian Sunset." There were purples, and blues, and shades melting into black. It was really quite pretty. I mean, it hurt like hell, but it sure looked nice. I hadn't slept well the previous night, so I was looking forward to hopefully getting some rest tonight—after my milkshake of course. One of our good friends had taken the lead and set up a meal train for Erin and the girls. It was nice that with everything Erin was dealing with, at least meals were being handled. And the girls didn't have to hunt and gather. As another small victory, today was Emma's last day in true quarantine. Erin and Rachel had continually tested negative for COVID, and Emma was now almost done. It had been an exhausting week, and we still had one more day of appointments on the twenty-second, which was also Emma's 18th birthday. But that was all to come. For today, they ate food generously provided. I had a milkshake and was asleep by six thirty. My body and my spirit were tired, but I had miles to go…

January 22

Nights are the hardest. I lie in bed thinking, often too much. I am constantly accompanied by the gentle in and out sounds the oxygen compressor makes as it takes and converts room air into pure O2. It lives downstairs in the front room, so that the hose can reach the entirety of the house. Not that I am going through the whole house. I stay in my room all day, only coming out to go to appointments. I lay in bed at night and think back. I close my eyes, and in certain moments I can picture myself in places our family has visited. For a moment, my hands are touching the slot canyon walls of Zion National Park as we walk through the river. For a time, I'm riding shotgun on Kauai with my hands out of the window feeling the air. I can smell the flowers. I can hear the ocean. Briefly, I am holding one of my girls in my arms in some undetermined, and unimportant, location. And then it's over, and I am back in my bed. In those short trips, I am alive again. Returning to the present, I am dying. This is true, and I am starting to come to the realization that the end is approaching faster than we think. Our time is short on this planet as it is. Right now, the only thing keeping me here is this oxygen and my determination. I'm not ready to visualize the future. All I have is what is behind and what I have today. Today, I have to return to Chapel Hill.

Today is Emma's 18th birthday, too, and her quarantine is over! Not wanting to break with tradition, I had Erin go to the local bagel store to order the Emma special. Silly? Sure. Beyond the Emma special, I'm not really sure what we did for her birthday. My memory at this point is starting to have gaps in it. I suppose my body was too busy surviving to try to imprint things on my long-term memory. Erin and I loaded the car—though by

"Erin and I," I really mean Erin and the girls, making sure everything was there. We were getting smarter about our packing though. After the debacle of not having food after the cardiac cath, we started to pack a small cooler with drinks and snacks. We would not be caught unprepared again. Rachel would help me get to the car, Emma would turn off the compressor to give it some much-needed rest, and Erin would have the car ready. Our packing list looked like this by now:

- Oxygen, and lots of it
- Oxygen cart with room for two bottles
- Extra cannula
- Cooler
- Snacks and drinks
- Book bag containing:
- Snacks
- Books
- iPad
- Nintendo Switch
- Device chargers
- Phone/wallets/keys

In the words of Bubba from *Forrest Gump*, "And, that's all there is." It was enough, especially when you consider Erin had the bag on. We'd attach the cooler to the handles of the wheelchair, and I had figured out a way to put the oxygen cart on the footrests. Add those two bottles to the bottle slot on the chair, and I had enough air for about three hours. I can only imagine the effort it took Erin to get me around that damn place. But she did it, and not once did she complain. Her dedication and commitment were limitless.

Our appointments today were with nuclear medicine and back in the transplant clinic with the doctor, the dietician, and social worker. I bet you can guess how our arrival went by now:

"No, I've not been around anyone with COVID."

"No, I've not tested positive."

"No, I've not been out of the state."

"Well, yes, I do have a cough and shortness of breath, but they aren't COVID related."

To which the gatekeeper replies:

"Here's your mask. You may proceed."

Once arriving at check in:

"No, I've not been around anyone with COVID."

"No, I've not tested positive."

"No, I've not been out of the state."

"Well, yes, I do have a cough and shortness of breath, but they aren't COVID related."

Every. Single. Time.

Clearing the Spanish Inquisition again, we took the elevator downstairs back to the radiography waiting area. By now, we were calling it the DMV and would continue to do so for the rest of my journey. Today's visit to nuclear medicine was all about my kidneys and how good they are. There would be scans, the injection of some type of radioactive material, more scans, and even blood draws. All of these had to occur on a very specific schedule. There would be lots of back and forth from the fourth-floor clinic to the DMV.

According to my records, this is what they did:

"2 1-second images, 25 15-second images, and 1 60-second image of the abdomen and pelvis (including the injection site) were obtained. Regions of interest were drawn around both kidneys and split function was calculated. Following injection of radiopharmaceutical, serum samples were obtained at 1 hour and 3 hours, and normalized counts utilized to calculate GFR."

GFR stands for glomerular filtration rate. According to the National Institutes of Health, "A **GFR** of 60 or higher is in the **normal range**. A **GFR** below 60 may mean kidney disease. A **GFR** of 15 or lower may mean kidney failure." They also consider a normalized GFR to be 145.07 mL/min. Happily, all of my tests would come back in the normal range. My GFR was 160.09 mL/min. My kidneys would not hold up this process. Kidney issues, I would learn, often accompany a lung transplant. Medicines play a role in this, so it was important to make sure that my kidneys were doing as they should in the pre-transplant phase. In the hospital I would also learn just how seriously they take this.

Careful examination of my chart reveals that I had another nuclear medicine test performed on this day too. I have absolutely no memory of this test occurring, though Erin seems to. Clearly it happened, as there are results of them checking the perfusion of my lungs. I guess I passed this test too, as I moved forward.

Our trip to the fourth floor transplant clinic that day was a real non-event. The meeting with the social worker was more or less a rehash of everything we had already discussed. The meeting with the dietician was a little more involved. My celiac issues were heavily discussed and we talked at great length about how my dietary needs in the hospital would be addressed. I would, in time, meet with the director of food services and the head chef for the hospitals. I would be taken care of as well as possible. Everything was being done to ensure my safety from a food standpoint. Truly, this was a team effort. I had no idea how many people were involved in this and how many tests I would have to endure to even possibly, just maybe get new lungs.

We're able to leave the hospital in a fairly reasonable amount of time. It's been quite a week. Not only am I physically exhausted from being poked and prodded, but mentally and emotionally this is all taxing. You try to stay positive and not let doubts creep in. We've crammed appointments that would normally stretch over months into an incredibly short period of time. The doctors have been impressed with my stamina and have told me that this speaks to my overall strength and determination. My efforts have shown them that I am willing to do whatever is asked of me. Hell yes, I am. I mean to keep on living. We have almost reached the finish line on pre-transplant evaluation. On Tuesday we'll return to meet with the pharmacist and surgeon. We'll see my nurse coordinator as well. At that point, once insurance approves (typically same day, could be up to 48 hrs), I'll be listed. The hope is that my wait will not be long. I'm tired, and so is Erin. She has lugged stuff, pushed me all over that dang hospital, joined me at appointments, managed to work some, and been a great companion throughout. She has also gotten way better at driving the wheelchair! The good news is we get three much needed days off.

January 26

One step closer. With each day, appointment, and test, I get one day closer.

Today we head back to Chapel Hill for three meetings. We started our day with our lightning quick exit at valet. It was good that we've gotten so smooth with this, as today it was 42 quickness and get to where we need to be in a moment. No small feat given all the crap we're lugging. I refuse to type the COVID questions again, but rest assured, they were asked. Once checked in, we ventured up to the transplant clinic and were shown to a room where I was able to hook up to all the oxygen I could stand.

Our first meeting was with the pharmacist. She went over the various medicines that I'd be taking post-transplant—and some of them for the rest of my life. Prior to all of these pre-transplant evolutions, we had received a book describing the entire process from the folks at UNC, so we'd already read about many of the medications. She told us of the benefits and need for the medicines as well as potential side effects, and asked about my ability to remember to take medicines and keep current on what to take and when. For some of these medicines, taking them at the same time each day is extremely important. None of this information was all that out of the ordinary or new, as we had read the book. The pharmacist was very nice though, and I'm glad we established a good rapport, since I'll be dealing with her for the foreseeable future. After this first meeting ended we hung out in the same room and waited for the next one.

A side benefit of going to the clinic is that everyone comes to you. It's a fairly efficient way of doing things and they have it down pretty good. We didn't have to wait all that long before meeting with one of the nurse coordinators. She went over some logistics, like how the process moved from this point forward, what would happen when I got "the call," things like that. The real development from her visit was that I signed some paperwork. The simple kind of stuff you sign when you're trying to have surgery to replace a major organ. Essentially, giving consent to move forward while noting that I understood the risks associated with a transplant, including potential death. It's funny though: when you are actively staring death in the eye and you get paperwork that mentions death as a "possible outcome," you sign with alacrity. It was the easiest time I ever had signing something. The way I saw it, I was dying already. This was certain. The benefits far, far outweighed any risks.

Next we moseyed from the transplant clinic to the cancer hospital to meet with the surgeon. One thing I started to realize was that there's no real rhyme or reason as to why people and clinics are where they are in the hospital. Or maybe there is. Maybe it's unknowable. Anyway, we met with the thoracic surgeon. In a word, he was awesome. He was knowledgeable and had a great sense of humor that put me at ease. He described the surgery (comparing it to opening the hood of a car), the recovery, and the risks. I asked if there were any concerns he had about my specific case, given what he knew, and he said no. He said he was ready to rock. I sheepishly asked if there would be any way there could be pictures taken during the surgery. He said this wouldn't be a problem. I only had to provide a disposable camera and they'd make it happen. I thought it'd be neat to see what my old lungs looked like, and what the new ones look like. It turns out, we'd see more. A lot more. We left Chapel Hill, and for the first time in a while I felt optimistic. I had passed every test needed, impressed every person that mattered (all of 'em), and fought through a challenging time.

Once we got home, my actual coordinator called and said she was starting the paperwork for insurance to approve the transplant. Once I completed my last two appointments the following day, she would submit the paperwork. Her rationale was that there was no reason or any sign that there would be anything that would cause me to hit a snag at this point. I would also have to get a COVID test. She had given herself a deadline of Friday the twenty-ninth to get me listed. The prevailing sense I got from everyone was that no one seemed to think I'd be on the list long.

The process was moving fast. I was told again—by a different person than last week—that the fact that I was able to handle everything they threw at me spoke to my grit, my tenacity, and my overall fitness (minus the crappy lungs). Essentially, I'm stubborn. Sometimes a character trait like stubbornness can be a character flaw if you let it become too prevalent in your life. In this case it would pay off for me.

It's weird thinking about how quickly life can change for you. None of us expected this. When we started down this road in September of 2020, the prevailing sense was that I'd start some medicines and we'd see how things go. No one expected me to step off of a cliff in December. It really felt like the transplant team was going above and beyond. It was almost like the doctors took it personally that I got so sick, so quickly. I'm glad they did.

January 27

The last day of testing. As I completed the most important couple of weeks I would ever experience—well, to this point—I was reminded of an experience I once had. I've had the great opportunity to travel to Cuba on several occasions. I was able to travel there before many restrictions had been lifted, so I got to see and experience some interesting things. On one of the trips, I was on a small albatross (charter plane) flying back home from Havana to Miami. To begin with, we were weighed before getting on the plane and assigned seats in such a manner to balance the plane. It must be important that the plane not list to one side. Maybe if it did it would only fly in a circle? The two guys in the front, who I assumed to be the pilots, looked a bit sketchy. My confidence was not high. As we were heading to the runway, they stopped the plane, opened the windows, and got some kind of instructions. The flight across the shark-infested Florida Straits was a non-event, but one thing about an albatross is that they are not good at landing. These two "pilots" landed the plane, skidded sideways into a stop, looked at each other, and then high-fived. This story is absolutely true and anyone else who was on that flight will confirm it. I took that to mean that this was their first successful landing. This is much the same way I finished all of my testing—I skidded to a stop, looked at the pulmonary therapist, and high-fived her. I was glad to have successfully landed.

The day itself was not particularly long, but it was exhausting just the same. We went back to UNC where our expertise in navigating valet and check-in was on full display. Our first sign that this day was to be a bit odd started at check-in. The lady at the check-in desk was experiencing what I can only describe as COVID fatigue. After the requisite COVID questions (again) she started on what could only be called a rant. It was hard to completely make out her complaints through her mask, but there was a lot of mentions of Wal-Mart. Once we were able to peel away from her, we headed back to the transplant clinic (where they check me in by sight now) to meet with the infectious disease doctor.

This doctor was … interesting. I can only imagine what it must be like to go through life as an infectious disease doctor. Everything must look like a virus or a fungus or a bug. It must be horrible. I wonder if his house is hermetically sealed? For the most part I wear a bunch of black and gray t-shirts to go with my more sensible choice of sweatpants. Who says we can't learn and grow? Comfort was key. I decided that for these visits, I would add some color. I wore a burgundy shirt Emma got for me at the Grand Canyon in 2019. The doctor saw it and asked if I had been there. I didn't realize it was a trick question. When I replied that I had been there three times and enjoyed hiking, his fungus alarm must have sounded. He wanted to add another blood test for some fungus that is prevalent in the desert southwest. I guess he thought I spent a good portion of my year in the desert southwest. In fact, the notes from that day mention frequent travel to that part of the country. I haven't been there in six years. He asked of my travel history and each place I mentioned garnered some kind of perceived judgement. You would have thought I told him that I liked to drink water from stagnant ponds or something. It was weird. I need to give him the benefit of the doubt. We were in the middle of a pandemic and he deals in bugs and whatnot, so he has to be wired a bit differently. At the end of the visit though, he said we were good to go on his end. This put us one step closer.

After this visit we went to get my COVID test done. Once I got the call, they'd do one in the hospital, but since the idea was that I was going to get the call soon, they wanted a negative baseline. I'd get the results later in the day.

We had some time to kill before my final visit, and we were able to enjoy lunch together. Erin took us to a Jason's Deli, where we placed an online order and then enjoyed our lunch in the safe confines of our car. The two of us had been on the go so much, it was nice to take a moment and slow down. Being in the moment was something I was getting better at. It's easy to do when all you have is the moment.

We got to the pulmonary rehab clinic in plenty of time. This clinic was the one I'd visit after transplant for my rehab so it was nice to find it. It was also nice that it was just off of I-40 and across the street from the new Wegman's. I'd have to visit this clinic three times a week for about 10 weeks, so whoever drove me could go to Wegman's: win-win. I was originally supposed to do this visit on the day of my cardiac cath, but we remember how that went. Usually this clinic visit was the first of them all. It established whether or not you were fit enough to begin the process. I mentioned this was my last thing, right? If you don't meet minimums, they put you on a plan to get you ready. There are lots of people who are still trying to meet minimums.

The therapist was great. She mentioned how out of the ordinary this was, but she understood that there was lots of urgency. She also mentioned that this would be hard for me coming at the end of a hard week, but given what I had already done, she felt good. She hooked me up to 30L of oxygen and we were off. Test one was to stand up and sit down in a chair as many times as I could in 30 seconds without using the armrest. The goal was 12. I made 19—crushed it. Next, I had to stand from a chair, walk a short distance, and sit back down. The goal was 12 seconds. I did 7.1 seconds—feeling good. Last item up, the dreaded six-minute walk. I thought I was done with "1,000 feet in six minutes." For lots of folks this is a deal breaker. I don't know why this time and distance is so esteemed, but apparently it's the gold-standard. As it turned out, the six-minute walk I'd done in the hospital earlier was the one that truly mattered in terms of getting listed. This one was supposed to be a starting point. It would make perfect sense that I did it last of all—nothing about my journey had been normal to this point.

Anyhow, off I go. I start at a record breaking pace, which is good, because with one lap to go, she has to replace one of the O2 bottles. The time doesn't stop! Come on, lady! If I had to take a break, I'd understand keeping the clock moving, that's on me. This is not. Stop the damn clock!! No dice, the time kept slipping by. I look down the hall, I look at the watch, I see seconds ticking by, and I start to gauge when I'll have to run. I complete half of the last lap, see that I have seconds to go, and as I skid to a stop in the chair at the end, six minutes elapsed, we've flown over shark-infested water, we've touched down, and we high-five each other. This albatross has landed. I'm done. The testing is over. There is nothing more I can do. I have made every effort to get on the transplant list.

I received an email that my paperwork had been submitted to insurance. Once they approved, I'd be listed. It now came down to my lung allocation score. Based on my oxygen needs, blood type, and body size, I'd get a score. The higher the score, the better my chances of getting lungs sooner rather than later. I told the nurse I wanted to score in the 90s. She told me I didn't want that as it usually meant I was more or less dead. She said she'd be pleased with a score in the 60s. A score there would make me competitive and hopefully get me going.

This whole process had been something. It was hard to wrap my head around all of this. I'd gone from being a more or less healthy middle-aged guy to the verge of death in a matter of months. I'd always been active. I'd always had plans and looked forward to things. Now, I was just trying to get from one moment to the next. I chuckled at one point and Erin asked why I was laughing. In this entire process, I'd not shed one tear, so I imagine a chuckle was out of the ordinary. I told her that I was just thinking that this was not the way I had planned for my life to go. True, I'd never really had normal life plans. I'd just always assumed I'd be able to navigate the years in a normal way and do whatever seemed cool. But life throws all of us challenges. My challenge is my challenge, and one thing I've learned is that no one's challenges are any greater or less than anyone else's, they're simply their own. We can only navigate our challenge as best as we can.

Oddly, I have had absolutely no interest in trying to connect with other folks in the transplant process. Their journey is not my journey. Their challenges are not mine. Their successes are not mine, and nor are their failures. I can only travel my road. I received a text this week from a friend that gave me pause. He said that "I was tough, and that all I've been through to this point would help me get over this hill." That made me feel good. After all, he was on that charter flight from Cuba, and we got through that. I've also long told the girls that life is going to give us challenges and things won't always go to plan. How we respond shows who we are. I hope I'm providing a good example. I would be given plenty of chances to respond to challenges over the next few weeks.

January 29

It's official. I'm officially listed for transplant. Wow, that feels weird to type. My lung allocation score is 57.6587, which is very competitive. My nurse told me to keep my phone handy and the ringer on. Getting to this point has been the result of the hard work of a ton of people: the medical folks, schedulers, parking folks, the oxygen people, and especially Erin. Now, we wait. We don't know how long, but it's all I can do. This brings up something that I've not yet touched on. As excited as I am to be listed and potentially fixed in just a few days, my gain is dependent on the immeasurable loss for another family. It really kind of brings this whole thing into focus. For now, I won't dwell on that. I will focus my energy on not driving myself mad while waiting. So for today, there are no jokes. No witty observations. No fun stories. There is only relief at being listed and cognizant of what that means.

February 2021

February 1

It's difficult to remember just how alone I was in those days. Not difficult as in "man, I can't remember," but difficult to think about me being in that situation. February 1 was day three of being on the list to receive a transplant, but the wait had already been brutal. Three days. Brutal. Ha. Man, if I had only known what was to come, I think these days wouldn't have seemed so long. But, we are not gifted with the benefit of foresight. There's no way to know what joys or disappointments wait just around the corner, and as it turns out, there would be plenty of both in my very near future.

At this point in my descent into death, I spent the vast majority of my time in my room. My room was my sanctuary. Since a positive COVID test could derail everything we'd sought to accomplish, I was living a fairly solitary life. Occasionally someone would open the door to speak, bring me some food, and otherwise check on me. For the most part, though, it was me, books, the web, TV, and a Nintendo Switch. Whenever someone opened the door, I would get excited. And if an outsider (gasp!) came to visit, I was ecstatic. Well, as ecstatic as I could get at this point. Rachel was clear of her COVID quarantine at this point, so I'd occasionally get a visitor who didn't live in my house. My parents would come by, a couple of our good friends would drop in to check on me, my in-laws came by once and visited, but that was it. Besides that, I was playing Nintendo and watching the Simpsons. My mother-in-law expressed her displeasure at the show, much as she did when I was a teenager. I thought, "God, woman, I'm not 17 anymore." Maybe she still sees me that way. Maybe my parents still see me as a boy. I suppose when we look at people, we see what we remember about them best (or first).

I remember looking in the mirror around this time and wondering what was staring back at me. I did not recognize that person anymore.

Back to our programming...

The day before, the doorknob turned and Emma kicked open the door. She informed me of a poor grade she'd received on an assignment and expressed her general consternation at the whole situation. I asked her; "What can you do today to try and make the problem better?" She answered and I told her to go do that thing and then let it go. This is how I was now trying to deal with the wait to receive a phone call. "What can I do today?" And right now, the answer was not a dadgum thing. Life kept happening all around me. I could see it on social media and in my own house. Rachel was waiting for soccer try-outs. Emma had been accepted into East Carolina University. They were both planning to return to on-campus learning. Emma was even going to get a version of a football season this year. Games would begin at the end of the month. Things were coming.

But we can only wait for these events to happen in our lives. It's a little easier when we know they're coming and we can plan for it. A graduation, a wedding, heck, even a birth—you know it's on the horizon and you can prepare. With Emma's birth, we were able to plan, prepare, and swing by to get a bagel. Heck, even with Rachel's quick arrival, all of our ducks were in a row. We were prepared, I just had to hurry Erin to the hospital. For me, with my situation, I was stuck in an endless loop of the same day. This has to sound like the bitching of a person with no patience whatsoever. It's true, I'm not patient. But I'm not complaining either. It was hard, but it was still manageable at this point.

My entire life had spun completely out of control at this point. This was hard, particularly for someone who likes to have at least some semblance of control. Never, never did I think that the wait would be so hard. I figured that the testing would be hard (it was), or that the transplant would be hard (it would be), or that rehab would be hard (eh), but I did not think that sitting and waiting would be so very brutal. I think the reason why it was so damn tough is that this part was 100% out of my hands. There was absolutely nothing I could do to speed up this process. But I'd control what I could control. For the moment, that was how much I read, *Super Mario Bros.* or Super Mario 2, *Simpsons* or *Family Guy*, socks or not, shower today or shower tomorrow (Erin voted for both). "This is all I can do today, so I'll do it." If the call came in the meantime, so be it. If not, I'd get up and do it all again the next day. I was starting to get concerned that I might get to the end of the internet or Netflix though...

If I knew that I would get a call on Thursday, then we could mentally prepare for that. Not only was I waiting for a call, I was waiting for major surgery as well. It was a slippery slope, this. Speculating when something might happen only led to more disappointment with each passing day. I'd go to sleep thinking, "tonight is the night," only to wake up disappointed that it didn't happen. Maybe this was part of the greater journey I was on. I was learning that there were lots of things I couldn't control. We can only do what we can, in that moment, to get through whatever struggle we are in. It was hard keeping this in perspective—understanding it and being OK with it were two very different things. The wait was not getting any easier.

February 5

One reason I wasn't overly interested in speaking with other transplant patients about their stories at this point was that I didn't want the negativity. To be fair, most everyone I'd talked to who was either waiting for their transplant or had already gotten it was overly optimistic and friendly. However, I did not, in any way, want to hear from the person who had been listed for months. I did not, in any way, want to think about being confined in my room for months waiting for my call. I wanted to get back to living. It should be noted that if they were waiting that long, then their score wasn't that high, and there were reasons. It goes back to the great question of clinic locations in the hospital. Maybe there is a reason, maybe not. Sometimes things just … are.

My wait was becoming interminable, never-ending, brutal, painful, any word you can conjure to express difficulty would work. Reflecting back on it now, it is becoming hard to remember just what a struggle it was. But even though the memories are fading, I know. I was getting more and more down by the day. When we're in the moment, it's hard to understand just how short these time frames can be. February 5 was a Friday, and it marked my one week "anniversary" of being listed. One week. It had only been one week. At the time, it felt like the second coming would occur before I got the call. I suppose if that were the case, the call would've been a moot point …

I tried to describe the wait to someone in a way that anyone who has ever had kids could understand. When Emma and Rachel were babies, they were good babies. They never really gave us problems, as best as I can remember. It was the overall "newness" of it all. It would be feeding time, I'd get up, get the baby, bring her to Erin, and they'd do their thing. After they were done, I'd take them back to their room, change them, and put them back to bed. It was a team effort. But after a week or two, it started to seem like they would never sleep through the night. In hindsight, I don't remember it being all that long. That's life, isn't it? Once upon a time, I was carrying my new daughter to her mother. Now, I was carrying her to college. The time in between was not that long.

Each day I woke up and put one foot in front of the other. We, and I mean all of us in this house, were just trying to get by. In school, at work, medically, we were just trying to make it. And it was getting harder.

One of the requirements of the transplant process was to participate in bi-monthly group chats with the social worker and other folks listed or post-transplant. I am not much of a group therapy person, as mentioned. I just had to play the game. The group workshop for this week was a real knee slapper. The session was on potential complications from transplant. The list is long and filled with all kinds of wonderful maladies, including death! What a hoot! I'm *this* close to actually going under the knife and that's the session. You know what? Honestly, I didn't care. For some folks, I think they default to thinking about what might go wrong in this process. For me, I've never cared about potential complications. The way I was looking at the prospect of complications was simple. If something came up, that meant I'd had the transplant and survived. We could always fix stuff at that point. I trusted that, whatever might happen, the doctors had seen it before and could handle it. I was in competent, caring hands.

The weather had matched my mood now for a few days. It's hard to keep a sunny disposition when it's cold and rainy outside. Early February in North Carolina can be beautiful, or not. That week, it had not been. The world outside my window appeared dead and lifeless. It most definitely mirrored my body and spirit. What I was doing at this point wasn't living, it was maintaining. Confined to my room, I was slowly turning into a recluse, and it wasn't fun. I hadn't yet put aluminum foil over the windows or renounced all personal hygiene, but I was becoming more and more isolated. It was getting to the point where I didn't have enough energy for visitors.

A really good friend of mine, the guy I would consider my best friend, had asked me what I was most looking forward to once this is over. My answer was simple: I looked forward to rejoining life. I looked forward to dinner with my family again, walking with my wife again, driving a kid (Rachel, at this point) somewhere, and just being present. As I sat there, a week since my listing, I was not good—but I was persisting. I was not living, but I was alive. I wasn't present, but I was there. I was getting used to things being out of my hands. I was getting used to learning to deal with hard days. Because I was learning to live in each day, I was facing each day with renewed hope. Each time my phone would ring, I would get excited. One of these times, I would have good reason to feel happy. My number would soon come up.

February 6

Oh, February 6. How can I accurately describe how absolutely shitty you were? How can I tell to all the world how you will forever be my least favorite day of the year? How can I put into words how you hurt me? Maybe I'm being too hard on you, February 6. You're just a day. It's not your fault. But I have to blame something.

Here's how Erin described the day:

"Today we had a ‹dry run.› We got the call at 1:15 a.m. to head to the hospital. We stayed in a room in the ER and met with plenty of doctors all morning. By one o'clock p.m., we were wheeled to the pre-op area. And all was ready until the surgeon came in at two p.m. to say that there was a spot on one of the lungs and he did not want to use them. It was heartbreaking, but we understood. We got home around three fifteen p.m. We are heading to bed soon."

A "dry run," you ask? What is a a dry run? It doesn't sound all that nefarious, but nefarious it is. A dry run is something that every lung transplant candidate needs to mentally prepare for. A dry run is when you get a call and they tell you to come to the hospital—you have some lungs. As you make your way to the hospital, the team dispatches a surgeon and other personnel to where the lungs are going to be found. You get to the hospital and wait while the lungs are, to be delicate, "obtained." The doctors look at scans and imaging before deciding if the lungs are OK. The only way to truly know, though, is to actually look at them with your eyes. If, after imaging and the eye test, the lungs are good, then and only then can you get them. While these decisions are being made, the potential recipient waits at the hospital.

With each step closer to transplant, the recipient changes locations-getting ever closer to the operating room. Any red flag along the way can stop the transplant cold. Every recipient is told that most people have a dry run or two. Intellectually, you understand this. Emotionally, it wrecks you. Erin's description is technically accurate. For me, there was more to the day. This is how I remember it …

I was in that place where you're not asleep but not awake either. It was 1:20 in the morning when my ringing phone sliced through the silence of our house. When I saw the Chapel Hill number, my heart leapt into my throat. I was so excited when I answered the phone my voice was quivering. On the other end, the nurse coordinator told me it was time. They had a set of lungs and needed us to make our way to the hospital. Since Erin was still sleeping in the bonus room, I called her and roused her and we started to get ready. No rush, I was told—just be there by three or so. Everything felt like it had a "last" attached to it. This was my "last" shower as a sick person. My "last" ride as a sick person. We got ready and I got the girls up to give them a hug. My "last" hug as as sick person. Traffic was light (it was two a.m.) and we were at the hospital around two thirty.

Because of my oxygen requirements, we were told that I was to go to the Emergency Room to wait, so that's where we went. The parking guy was super nice, as was the receptionist. Mercifully, the ER waiting area was a ghost town, and once we got through the metal detector we were taken to our private room to wait. We passed through the area with people in all manner of distress and were shown to our room. Our room was across from the bathroom, had a proper door, and even a TV. We waited for them to finish cleaning the room and then got settled. The donor surgery was not set to happen until around noon, so we had some time to wait. I had some blood drawn and a COVID test done. The blood draw was easy, and I'd had a COVID test done several times, but this one—good grief. I'm fairly sure she hit my brain stem, that she was elbow deep in my nose, and that the fluid that leaked out was in fact cerebrospinal fluid. Holy moly. All of this was before four. It would be hours before we saw anyone else. In the emergency room, I was not emergent. My needs did not take precedence over those people who were in true distress. There's always someone worse off, right?

Around eight, my surgeon came by. One glitch, though: it wasn't the surgeon I had met with. He was on vacation until the seventh. There were three surgeons who did lungs here, and there was a strong chance that all of them could have a hand in me. Literally. This one seemed fine. He was competent and would do a fine job, but I was really at ease with the other. At any rate, this wasn't a deal-breaker—it wasn't like I was going to walk out. He talked a bit, told me that I was pretty much at the top of the list in our region, and that we were just waiting for perfect lungs. He said these looked OK, but there was one area of concern and that we wouldn't know for sure until they were removed from the donor. He left, and I saw one of my pulmonologists, who suggested we add an hour or two to the noon projection.

The morning passed, we did a Zoom with Erin's family, and nothing much happened. Preparing for a transplant involves lots of "hurry up and wait." We were in the waiting phase. Around noon, the nurse came in and said they'd be down soon to take me to get ready for surgery. A few minutes later a friendly orderly showed up to take me from the ER to pre-op. He really was nice, and at this point I was feeling fairly optimistic. I had called my parents and had my head in the proper place for what I thought was coming.

Medical transport got me to pre-op, and since it was a Saturday afternoon, I was the only one there. We met with the anesthesiologist, I signed more consent forms, and I could see the door to the operating area. I was feet away. They told me it was time to get out of all my clothes, put on my hairnet, and wait. I called my girls to tell them I loved them, and as I was speaking to them, the surgeon walked in. The look on his face was not good. He said the gasses on the lungs were good, but … But there was a spot. There was a spot on the underside of one of the lungs. It showed on the CT scan and was confirmed with visual inspection. He wanted to turn them down.

He wanted perfect lungs. He was the expert. Minutes from surgery and feet from the room, everything came crashing down. Everything.

I cried. For the first time in this entire journey, I cried. It wasn't a gentle cry. I was sobbing. Erin had tears. The nurse in pre-op had tears. The surgical fellow had tears. Everyone understood the need to wait. We're all smart people and we get it. What I wasn't ready for was the emotional side. I was so damn close. I had spent the entire morning getting my head right. I was scared, I was excited, I was anxious—you name it, I felt it. I was cautiously optimistic all morning long. I had even managed a few moments of genuine excitement. The staff tries hard to manage expectations, but once I got to pre-op and they took off my clothes, I was ready for whatever was on the other side of that door, physically and metaphorically. Now, all of that was gone. I have never experienced the swing of emotions that I experienced that day. It was gut-wrenching and crushing. I was devastated, and I was thirsty.

The nurse was really kind. She brought me something to drink and gave me time to process the first brush of emotions that was having. I wouldn't be right for days. Even as I sit here now I'm not sure that I've ever truly made my peace with this day. Erin helped me to slowly get dressed and transitioned me from my hospital bed to my wheelchair for the trip to the car. It was quiet car ride home.

We came home. I was greeted by my girls. Their faces reflected my mood. They helped me inside and I made my way back to my prison cell. Erin and I spent some time talking. After every crisis, some amount of debriefing is necessary. We had to confront what we had just experienced. We had to figure out how to make a silk purse out of a sow's ear. As crushing as this was, we tried to find positives. We had to look for the positives. To not do this would be to admit the day was a loss. As disappointing as it was, it wasn't a complete loss. We'd navigated the day with aplomb. Now we knew what to expect with each step of the process and how to deal with it. We learned what items were important to bring and which ones we wouldn't need. For example, Erin learned she needed two water bottles, not one. We learned that to the ER staff, I was just taking up space; if I needed something, I'd have to get it. We learned that over the course of my week of waiting, several sets of lungs had been turned down while they waited for the perfect fit.

It was comforting to know they had rejected lungs for me over the course of the week and I felt it would be soon that I'd get the call for sure. As I waited, I tried to picture what the day would be like, how I'd feel, what it'd be like to actually have it happening. No amount of imagining can prepare you for the emotions you feel when you think you're about to get lungs. So I was glad that I'd gone through that already. Next time, I wouldn't have to go through the full range of feelings. Trying to remain optimistic after February 6 was challenging. Right then, it sucked. I thought I'd be waking up that morning with new lungs. Sore, sure, but able to breathe. Instead I woke up as I had for the past month: alone and unable to breathe. It was OK though. I didn't want "OK" lungs, I wanted great ones.

February 12

Another week has passed here on Mt. Loneliness. I continued to spend most of the day in my room reading, watching TV, and basically just trying to pass the time. I really don't think anyone expected me to still be waiting at this point. I truly thought I would have been transplanted by now, but there I sat. Today was the first day where anything happened, and that was a follow-up visit. I guess I should also say that they did call on Monday, and I was excited, until I found out they only wanted to add another daily medicine. I pointed out that they really needed to quit toying with my emotions. In fact, the nurse on call should reach out to the person from some bat-phone kind of device. Something other than a regular Chapel Hill number.

Back to today. I have to be honest, I was in a foul mood. I was frustrated with having to be back going through all of the paces. I was frustrated at more blood work, more breathing tests, more EKGs, all of it. Frustrated. I was being short with Erin, short with everyone, and it was misplaced. I knew it but I just could not get out of it. They only needed one blood test done to check my CO_2 levels (still high), the EKG was easy, and I managed to somehow not have to do the six-minute walk and only had to do a pulmonary function test. Once I learned I wouldn't have to walk, my mood did pick up some. My lung function had dropped. I was at 26% function last month, now it was 25%. We went up to the clinic and met with a doctor, a nurse practitioner, and one of the transplant coordinators. It was a good visit. It felt more like a psychology session with a stethoscope. We left the appointment and I felt like I was at least a bit closer. My lung allocation score had increased, which was good, as it kept me closer to the top of the list.

So, yes, another week had passed and I was still waiting, though I felt a little more hopeful than I did. This had been quite the roller coaster ride, unlike anything I'd ever experienced. The weather hadn't helped either. I found myself thinking about things that were out of my hands. It happened when I first got to the hospital this morning. Going through the appointments was a good reminder to focus on what I could control. Once I did that (in fits and starts) it got better. And just like the weather, this storm would eventually pass. Maybe my next update would be in a different tone…

February 19

I'd now been waiting for my second call longer than I'd waited for my first. It took seven days for me to get a call for my dry run. That was two weeks ago. Two weeks. How in the hell did I get through these days? A better question—how in the hell did my family put up with me? An even better question—why did they put up with me? At this point I was starting to come to grips with the fact that it might not happen for me. I was beginning to slip into an even darker place.

As I sat here on Friday the nineteenth, it was a big nope. Not this week. Not so far, anyway. There had been no progress. It had been a cruddy few weeks, so maybe something good could help change the juju. Rachel was doing really well in school. Her grades were excellent, she was working hard and setting herself up for a successful high school experience. All of this while dealing with the shit show that was our life. The previous night she'd wanted to take a bath to "relieve stress." When asked what she had to be stressed about, her answer was perfect: "What don't I have to be stressed about?" But she was hanging in there and I was proud of her. Plus, Emma had had a chance to do some in person band things recently and had even seen a friend or two. She'd also found out that she'd gotten into the Honors College at ECU. To say that I was proud of these two is a vast understatement. Their spirit gave me hope.

Erin. I'm not sure what to really say about her. She was still my rock. There is absolutely no way I could have navigated this without her. She ran the house and her business and managed to keep me breathing and fed. I will never be able to thank her enough or show her how much it has meant to me. These three girls were the reason I kept hanging in there. They were the whole reason. We had much more to do together. Hanging in there was getting harder.

I was not in a great headspace. I was dumbfounded, confused, sad, lonely, bored, hurting, etc. I've never told anyone this or put it down before, but that was as close as I ever came to ending things. At that point, I just did not see any way out. I was getting sicker and sicker by the day. The struggle was becoming overwhelming. The only reason I didn't throw in the towel was because of my wife and kids. I wanted to see Emma graduate, I wanted to see Rachel go to prom. I wanted to travel with all of them again. I still wanted to do things. Trying to get my body and spirit to cooperate with each other was becoming almost impossible. I had now been listed longer than it took to get listed. My testing process was only about two weeks start to finish. I'd now been listed for three. I think everyone was in the same place—we all thought I'd have been transplanted by now, but there we were.

I am convinced that the doctors were waiting for the lungs of one of the Avengers to become available. Lungs like Thor's would be awesome, but at this point Ant-Man was looking good too. I knew the right ones would become available and I'd get the ones I needed. Intellectually I knew this, but emotionally, I was struggling. I tried to keep in mind that in a month or two, the wait would have been worth it. I kept envisioning some of the breaths I was looking forward to taking: my first deep breath in the mountains, at the beach, a good glass of wine, all of it. I kept thinking about walking in the woods without problems, or standing at a concert and singing along. It is truly amazing how much we take for granted. I don't remember a bunch of things from earlier in my life. Over the past few years, I've tried harder to really take in sights and sounds of places I experienced. Breathing in the air is now on that list. I was just ready. Who knows, maybe today would be the day the phone rang, and it would be my time … but I was beginning to doubt it.

February 21

It's funny the way things work out in life. You sit there on a Friday and bitch and moan about how long you're waiting, how bored you are, how depressed you're becoming. Then on Sunday morning at six thirty a.m. your phone rings. You sleep with your hand on your phone these nights because you don't want to miss that call. And I tell you what, I was so glad I had my hand on my phone: AT&T wanted to offer me the chance at lower rates! How did they ever know that this was exactly the call I was looking for? On a Sunday. At six thirty a.m. Grrrr. Once I was able to get my heart rate to settle back down to its now standard 120s, I turned on the TV.

It was another crappy weather day, and we thought that we'd treat the girls to dinner "out." In all honesty, we had been doing a fair amount of takeout for them while I kept drinking milkshakes. That and burgers and fries were the only things that tasted good. And peanut M&Ms. Tonight, though, it would be Japanese food and Chinese food. We called in the order and Emma went with Rachel to get the food. They got back home and set up what could only be called a buffet downstairs. Not that I was down there. Rachel made me a plate of lettuce wraps, fried rice, ginger chicken with broccoli. All of it. Not huge portions, mind you, but some of all of it. I was actually looking forward to eating for the first time in quite a while.

Rachel was in my room and my phone rang. It was a Chapel Hill number and Rachel froze in her tracks. From downstairs, I heard Emma yelling about "yum-yum sauce" or some such crap. Rachel hollered back that I was on the phone. It was time to come to the hospital. Rachel began to beam with excitement. One of our friends, who had come to hang with Erin, began to cry. I asked the nurse if I could eat my dinner.

I ate what I hoped was my "last" meal. I took another "last" shower. Got dressed in comfortable clothes for the "last" time. This time felt different than the time before. The air just hung heavy. After the dry run incident from earlier, we were all guarded in our optimism. Still, something just felt different. Even the hugs the girls gave me felt different. There was a feeling of love behind them. They were true hugs of love and not hugs of obligation. I can now recognize the difference. Emma told me as I left:

"Don't get any bright ideas about going off to join Scooter."

I couldn't help but smile and told her that as much as I loved that little dog, I was in no hurry to see him any time soon. After drying a few tears, Erin and I loaded up in the car and off to Chapel Hill we went. We arrived in Chapel Hill at eight p.m. for a projected surgery time in mid to late afternoon on the twenty-second. Erin and I settled in for a long romantic evening in the emergency room cardiac care bay five. After seeing Erin trying to cram onto the same hospital bed with me, the nurse even brought in an extra gurney for Erin to have her own bed. What a weird night.

February 22

The events were proceeding at a glacial pace, at least as I saw it. Neither Erin nor I was able to get much sleep the night of the twenty-first. Neither of us wanted to get our hopes up, and we were both staying balanced, emotionally—that's how it looked on the surface, anyway. I know that I said that having experienced the dry run, I wouldn't run the gamut of emotions again, that I had already done that. I was wrong. My head was all over the place. I'm not an overly religious person. It's not that I don't believe, it's just that I don't know what to believe. Surely there are larger forces at play than the ones we see. Maybe? Maybe all we see is truly all there is. What I can tell you for certain is that as I lay there waiting for what would unfold, I became a true believer, in God, or science, or whatever was going to see me through. My mom and I had engaged in several conversations on the subject over the past few weeks. She tends more toward a faith-based approach, and that's fine, there is absolutely nothing wrong with that. For me, at this particular moment, I was trusting the science more. I was trusting in my doctors and all of their skill and expertise. In that moment, I realized that there was no wrong mantle to put your trust on in such a situation. Each person has to do what makes them most at ease. If that means pray, then pray away. If that meant watch TV, then watch TV. Do you, boo. Do you.

Eventually, after lots of blood draws and a few x-rays, we were moved back into the same room from our dry run. It was nice to have a door and a TV, since both were lacking in my previous "room." Well, technically there was a door, but it was glass and provided little privacy. And there we waited. We waited all morning. Because I was waiting for surgery, I wasn't being allowed to eat or drink anything. As the day wore on, that became harder, but I had no choice. Occasionally, someone would drop by and say hello. A doctor here, a fellow there, maybe a nurse, maybe a social worker. This time we did have the knowledge that even though the surgery time for the donor was around two p.m., we would have to wait an additional hour or so. Managing expectations became important in the wait and would be important in the recovery.

Morning became lunchtime, and lunch bled into early afternoon. We sat and sat, but at least we were together. Looking back on this time sitting and waiting with Erin, I have a hard time contemplating what she must have been thinking. It had to have been hard. I was scared to death but at the same time so anxious and ready to go I could hardly stand it. I was tired of being tired. I was tired of dying. I can only guess that she was tired of the same things. She and the girls were keeping our little train moving down the tracks, but they all had to be exhausted. And, though none of them have ever told me so, they had to be scared. Around three p.m., the nurse came and told me that I'd be heading up to pre-op soon. We had been down this road before. I was still trying to temper my expectations, but I was starting to fail. I was allowing myself to get hopeful again.

The same super friendly transport guy showed up and pushed me on my bed from the ER up to the fourth floor, I think. I know there was a ride, a hallway that afforded a view of the Morehead Bell Tower at UNC and Kenan Stadium, and then an elevator ride. Not for the first time I reflected that this was happening on the campus of the university that brought so much change and joy in my life. I'd come full circle. I also remember thinking, and this is true, that if this was the last I ever saw of the outside world, at least it was Carolina. And that is something else I've never shared before.

Once again in pre-op, I got undressed and changed into my "surgical outfit." I was sexy to be sure—sexy hospital gown (10 sizes too big), sexy no-slip socks (XXL of course), and a sexy pink hairnet. Add that to the cannula and general look I had, it's a wonder the nurses could control themselves. My surgeon showed up with a grin on his face. The lungs were ace. They were absolutely perfect, and everything was a go. There would be no dry run this time.

The next stop was the surgery. I called my parents first and told them we were on and I'd talk to them later. Then I called Emma and Rachel. How do you have a conversation with your daughters when you are about to go into surgery? How do you talk to someone for what may be the last time? What do you say? What do you not say? I was thrilled to speak with them. I was terrified it would be the last time. Not wanting their final memory of me to be one of sadness, I stayed as upbeat as I could. I mean, I was happy. I had finally allowed myself to feel something akin to joy at this point. I just wanted to talk to them again. I didn't say good-bye. I just told them I loved them and I'd talk to them on the other side. Erin and I had a final moment together. She looked me up and down and gave me a hug. Then, for the first time in over a month, we kissed and then said good-bye. Neither of us had any way of knowing where this might go.

Alone, I lay there. Alone with my thoughts. You try to clear your mind, but there is no way. I was taken from pre-op to one last pre-surgical area. Here, all of my IV lines were checked, the surgeon came by to give me one last thumbs up, and the anesthesiologist came by to talk me through that process. I had to sign one last round of consent forms and then wait. It felt like a very long time. It wasn't. Around five thirty p.m., they came and got me and wheeled me into the surgical room. I recognized the eyes of my team as they waited for me. There were people everywhere, and it was all for me. I was transferred from my bed to the surgery table. It was cold in there. Like really cold. I'm sure I engaged, or attempted to anyway, in some kind of witty repartee. And I'm sure the team laughed dutifully. They had to know I was terrified. Yes, I was terrified. Yet there was also a sense of calm at this point. I had done all I could to make this happen. I had endured tests, poking, scans, imaging, walks, PFTs, clinic visits—all of it—just to get here. The doctors and the entire team had worked tirelessly to get here as well. And now it all came down to the next few hours. Erin had gone home to eat dinner with Emma and Rachel. That was the right thing to do. They were probably just sitting down together as the anesthesiologist approached me and said:

"OK, just breathe normally…"

February 23

There has been a great deal of discussion in our house since February 22 about what day my "re-birth" day is. Is it the day the surgery began or the day the surgery ended? If you want to go with the day it began, fine, that would be February 22, around six p.m., if you like. If you prefer to go with the day it was completed, that would be February 23, around two thirty a.m. Personally—and it's my damn story—I go with the twenty-third. I think it makes for a nice connection to my actual birthday of November 23. Or maybe I should go with the twenty-second. Maybe both? I also thought using the twenty-third would make it easy to remember. Wanna know a secret, though? I don't think I'll ever forget. Ever.

Erin was at home in bed when the surgeon called her and told her that everything went well. I was in recovery, and there was no reason for her to come to the hospital at two thirty in the morning. She could go back to sleep and come on over around seven or so, which I'm told is what she did. The details of the next few days are going to be heavily reliant on Erin's perspective. I have some memories, and I'm going to add them, but so much of this will come from Erin's point of view as she observed the comings and goings in the Thoracic ICU.

From Erin:

"Ronald was doing really well. The new lungs were pristine, and the surgeons were extremely happy with them. He spent the morning sedated and he is on a ventilator which is totally normal and expected. After lunchtime, they started reducing some of the drugs to let him wake up. He was alert and indicated no pain other than annoyance at the breathing tube.

His arms were strapped down to keep him from accidentally pulling out the breathing tube and he tried sign language to communicate with me. The sign language didn't really work so I got a piece of paper and pen and he would write a word or two to indicate his thoughts."

From me:

Yes, this I remember. I remember the annoyance at being intubated. I remember having my arms strapped down. I also remember wanting desperately to communicate with everyone. And, if I remember correctly, the nurse was really cute, and I wanted to communicate with her and show her how witty I could be. Looking at those strips of paper now is hilarious.

Erin: "Mostly his thoughts were on the music selection from his Spotify or to let me know he wanted to turn on the TV. And he definitely wanted to control the remote. Occasionally, it was to scratch his nose or tell me his legs were itching. He still has his sense of humor, and while he cannot laugh, I got a few smiles or thumbs up."

Me: Also true. All I wanted to do was listen to music and it felt like I couldn't get her to understand what I was trying to say. I was trying to write "Frank Turner" as hard as I could. Again, looking at it now, I don't have any idea why she couldn't decipher the chicken scratch of a semi-lucid post-double-lung-transplant patient. I mean, come on. How hard could this be? I do remember wanting to scratch all of the time. I don't remember wanting the TV remote, but I'm sure I did. My mind was an absolute soup at this particular moment, so anything I might remember could just be part of the "fog of war." What else does she say about this particular day?

Erin: "Mid-afternoon, they tried to reduce the drugs even more to get him more alert, and his pain level went up quite a bit. They have to have him awake to pull the breathing tube, but they do not want him in pain. And the plan is to remove the breathing tube and immediately give him an epidural. So, all afternoon it was a dance between controlling the pain and keeping him awake and alert enough to pull the breathing tube. And they need his labs to indicate that he is doing fine on his own."

Me: Yeah, so, OK. I totally remember this part. They tried to lower the fentanyl to a point that would allow them to get the breathing tube out. I did not handle this well. They only lowered it by a small, small amount and I felt like my world was imploding. It was pain unlike anything I had yet experienced. It was good my arms were still strapped down. Erin tells me that the look in my eyes resembled that of a cornered animal trying to break free. I could not communicate my pain verbally. It was all in my eyes. The decision was made to increase the fentanyl back to where it was and wait. Hey, Erin. What comes next?

Erin: "At 5:45 p.m. they did some lab work, and there was one number that was not quite right—nothing abnormal, just something they wanted to keep a watch on. So at that point, the doctors made the decision to leave the breathing tube in overnight and sedate him enough to keep him comfortable and try again in the morning. He understands their decision, but he is ready to have that breathing tube out. He is breathing on his own and the tube is there if they need it—especially in the overnight hours. So, they sedated him and he waved me goodbye and I came home for the night."

Me: That about sums up the day. Once they had me calmed back down and comfortable, Erin left, and I was alone. At least as alone as I could be in ICU.

February 24

February 24 was quite a day, as my healing continued. I never thought so many highly educated people would be so interested in when I was going to fart. It almost got silly how many times I was asked if I had done so. I would've been embarrassed being asked this by everyone if absolutely every bit of shame wasn't already gone. Let's briefly recap where I had tubes coming out of my body as this morning began.

I had:

- A breathing tube

- A central line coming out of my neck

- An IV in my left arm

- Four chest tubes draining

- One catheter … you know where

- A nasal cannula

- An NG tube in my nose

That about covers it. There was only one hole on my body without a tube, and not many more places left to poke, jab, or cut. Thanks to the pain meds, I wasn't in all that much pain. In fact, I didn't understand all the concern about pain. I was feeling OK. Overnight, they left me sedated to try and get as much rest out of me as they could, and as morning was breaking over beautiful Kenan Stadium, they began to lower the sedation to prepare to remove the breathing tube. I was glad that Erin could enjoy the view of the bell tower and stadium. While I had the line in my neck, I couldn't turn my head; I could only look straight ahead.

Around four a.m., the x-ray folks came in to take their images. The fellows were there early as well, and the decision was made to get me breathing on my own. Apparently I was more or less already doing so, but it was time to get that tube out. I started to mark my progress by the removal of things from my body. When Erin got to the hospital, the breathing tube was still in, but not for long. By ten a.m., they had come in and removed the tube. I was breathing, on my own, unassisted, without anything, and it was terrifying. It wasn't the way I imagined it would be. I thought I would have some great epiphany about how great and easy I was breathing. Nobody tells you that you're going to have to re-teach yourself how to breathe. For so long, I had been struggling to take any breath. It was like being underwater with someone standing on my chest. Now, that was gone. Just … gone. My last breaths were short and halting and rapid. Now I was being told to take deep breaths, and I could! I actually could! I would often, over the next few days, find myself falling back into my labored breathing patterns. I'd have to consciously tell myself to stop and remind myself that deep, normal breaths were possible.

After the tube was out, I was able to talk, and boy did I talk! There was serious discussion in the first few minutes of replacing the tube so the nurses and Erin could get some peace and quiet. I had lots to say. It had been a heck of a day or two. My voice was very raspy (more so than usual) but by the end of the day it was rounding back into shape. Perhaps I would become the songbird of our generation post-transplant. At the same time the breathing tube was pulled, the nurse mistakenly pulled out the NG tube as well. This tube was supposed to stay in until I had passed my "swallow test" (coming soon). However, she yanked that sucker right out and I didn't say a word. I was fine with it being out. I wouldn't need it.

The respiratory therapist started me on three liters of oxygen with the goal to wean me by the end of the day. I had been on 12 liters prior to surgery, so this was a great improvement. Around lunchtime, the surgeon who I think actually did most of the surgery came in to check on me. He saw the oxygen and cannula.

"Why do you have that?" he asked.

"Beats me, I just do what I'm told."

"Nope. I didn't put in new lungs for you to be hooked to oxygen."

"You're the doctor, " I said as he walked up to me and took the cannula from my head.

So, by one o'clock p.m., I had no oxygen support at all! For the first time since August, I was untethered to oxygen in any way. I was free and clear and breathing on my own.

Around the same time, the pain doctors showed up to give me my epidural. Funny, right? I get a breathing tube removed and another tube stuck in my back. The hope was to lower the narcotics that had been keeping me flying high and keep the pain under control with the epidural. The process was exactly the same as the one for expectant mothers. The main difference was that instead of aiming for a lower, more pelvic target zone, the epidural would be targeting my mid-chest. That makes pretty good sense. The doctors ran their fingers up and down my spine until they found what they were looking for, stuck a needle in there and threaded it (so to speak). The drip was set up in a lock-controlled box on my IV pole and I was given a button to release little extra boosts of medicine should I need it.

About two p.m., the physical therapist and occupational therapist came in and helped me get up from the bed. With the number of tubes I had coming out of my body and the number of containers and bags tied to those tubes, it took quite the team to get me up and walking. Here begins the story of my remarkable recovery. To this point I had been a fairly typical surgical case. Nothing big had popped up and everything was progressing as it should. Once I could start to take a little control of my healing, I was determined to get out as quickly as possible. I walked down the hall and back and they were thrilled with how far I went for a first effort. Don't let the bravado fool you, though. I was exhausted after the 50-foot walk, and once I got back to my room, I settled into my reclining chair for the remainder of the afternoon, and for most of the next 10 days.

Wednesday was starting to draw to a close. It had been an eventful day and one that had pleased the doctors and staff endlessly. My oxygen saturation levels were floating around 97–98%, higher than the hoped-for 90%. I was breathing on my own. I was filling up that bag with pee-pee, much to everyone's glee. The chest tubes were draining as they should, without an inordinate amount of fluid. I had walked. I was sitting up. I was on the mend. Now, I just had to start farting. Like I said, I was surprised how many people cared. My ability to become flatulent would show that my digestive tract was waking up from my sedation. This would be important so I could do a swallow test and begin to have food again. I had not eaten anything in over three days at this point. I was being nourished, sure, but I hadn't eaten. I was looking forward to the ability to at least have something to drink.

Erin went home for the evening to see the girls and have dinner, and I decided to stay in the ICU. It seemed like a good call. It was already becoming apparent to everyone that my time in the ICU proper would be short. I was progressing remarkably well. I was uncomfortable but not hurting. Resting was impossible, since I was being checked on with such frequency. I figured I'd rest once I got home. As darkness fell outside I was finally alone with my thoughts. Most of them centered around absolute amazement at my situation. I was in an ICU bed with tubes and monitors everywhere. And new freaking lungs! New lungs! How is this even a thing? Lots of my thoughts at this point were also focused on the physiological stuff I was going through: How to be comfortable. How to breathe. How to just function. There would be time to deal with the psychological side as I moved into the future. Because now I had a future. Two days ago, I did not. As I tried to get some sleep, I allowed myself to travel in my mind. Before transplant, I visited those places to try and relive happy memories. After it, I went there in anticipation.

February 25

It's good that I was able to travel in my mind. It was still impossible, absolutely impossible to get any rest whatsoever in the ICU. Looking back on it now, I suppose I was a little out of the ordinary in the unit. Most of the folks there were in far worse shape than I was. Most of them were either sedated or immobile. For them, it really didn't matter that the nurses and all other manner of folks were entering their rooms at all hours of the night. For me, I was most definitely not sedated and was fully aware of absolutely every single person who came and went from my room. Not that I had any control over it. Why should I have control now? I hadn't had control of my life for quite some time, so it was more or less life as usual. The night was a weird time and would continue to be so for the entirety of my stay in the hospital. Learning to breathe again was challenging. As I thought of happy places, I found myself breathing normally, taking regular, measured breaths. However, as I drifted off to "sleep," I'd start that shallow breathing crap again and wake myself up—scared. It was disconcerting; I felt like I just couldn't get a handle on how to breathe. It's a feeling I had never experienced and one I wouldn't wish on anyone.

There I was, all night long, lying face up in bed. All the tubes precluded me from much movement, and the line coming out of my neck made any type of head movement impossible. I couldn't lie on my side; I couldn't turn; all I could do was lie there on my back and look straight ahead. I did ask for something to help me get some rest, anything. I was willing to take melatonin, not that I expected it to help. I really wanted the good stuff. I just wanted to rest. No relief came. What did come was the x-ray technician. At three a.m.

Three in the damn morning! What the actual hell??? I couldn't figure out why in the world x-rays needed to be taken at three in the morning.

I could hear the technician coming. The mobile x-ray machine was an unwieldy creature. They'd wheel it into my huge room, position it, usually at the foot of my bed, place the board behind my back, and then snap the image. Then, poof, they were gone. As soon as they left, the nurse would usually come back in for my four-a.m. check. Then it was time to start getting me moved to the recliner. The doctors wanted me in the recliner as much as possible. Around five thirty, I'd hear the fellows outside of my room…

"OK, in here we have Mr. Campbell, double-lung, blah, blah, blah…."

"Guys, I can hear you…come on in and talk to me!"

Eventually, they'd enter the room and look at me. They'd ask how I was, listen to my lungs, check tubes, check my incision, and then leave. This would happen every day, both in the ICU and the step-down room, for the whole time I was at the hospital. And I found out why they took those x-rays so early. It was so they could have them before they started rounds in the morning. I guess there is a reason for everything. It's a lot like when you raise kids. They don't always understand our reasoning for things, we just assume we know best. I found through this process how important it was to understand why. Most times, if we know the why, then doing the thing is a little less objectionable. Either way, it was five thirty a.m., and I was already exhausted.

There was some good news from the overnight hours. My digestive system was starting to flex its muscles again. And by this, I mean I was farting. Like a champ. I don't know why I was so happy when I told my nurse about the first time it happened, but I was beaming. Weird things were making me happy. But each little step was one more step closer to normalcy. Let's keep in mind here that I was about two days removed from having my chest wide open. I was motivated. Life was moving on at home, and I wanted to get back to it. Emma had football games on the calendar, the most important one on March 26. That would be senior night, when the seniors in the band would be recognized with their parents at halftime. I was determined to be there. It was one month away and I had a long way to go. I'd have to get from the stands, walk the track, stand a while, and eventually walk the field. The prospect was a bit daunting at this point. But I was determined.

In fact, I was so determined to get out of the hospital that this morning, the twenty-fifth, I walked a pretty good distance. I managed to cover 300 feet. I know that doesn't sound like much. It's only a football field. But to me, I had just walked 50 miles. Before my surgery, I couldn't even get to the mailbox. Hell, going to the bathroom was too far. 300 feet, two days after surgery! I didn't get winded, and my oxygen levels stayed in the high 90s. Things were going great. The doctors were very pleased. The hardest part of the walk wasn't even the lungs: it was my legs. I just had absolutely no strength in them. They had started to weaken over the past couple of months and I would need some time to get the muscle back. But I covered the 300 feet with a walker and without a nurse pushing a chair behind me. Pleased as they were, the doctors decided that the arterial gas line in my left wrist could come out. Over time the dot would fade, but this was huge. I have said that any time something was removed from my body, it was a little victory. Well, here ya go. The day's little victory.

Doctors came and went throughout the morning. I'd see them all. Anyone who had a hand in my case would drop by: surgeons, pulmonologists, pain management, infectious disease doctors, nutritionists, social workers, etc., etc., etc. It was a revolving door, and while each doctor brought with them good tidings and good news, it was tiring. Since I was able to report a fair amount of "wind below," the doctors ordered the swallow test. If I was successful in this, I'd be able to take liquids and solids by mouth. If I was successful.

Spoiler ... I was successful. Because, of course I was. If it sounds like I'm tooting my own horn, well, I am. Around three thirty in the afternoon, my transport arrived to take me to have the swallow test. I can't remember how I was transported. It might've been a bed, it might've been a wheelchair. I'm leaning toward bed because of the sheer amount of stuff I had attached to me. Once I got down to the radiography lab (yep, the DMV) I was facing the same barium swallow as in my pre-transplant testing. On the counter, I saw all of the fluids I would be swallowing. Instead of a pill, like last time, this time I would swallow actual food with a barium "paste" on it.

"Is that a graham cracker?" I asked.

"Yes, we're going to put some barium on it for you," replied the technician.

"Yea, I can't eat that. I have celiac. Is there another option?"

"Oh. Umm. Let me see what we can do. Would an apple slice work?"

"Absolutely," I said.

Crisis averted. I was completely out of my head, still trying to get my legs and mind under me, and I was having to pay attention to my dietary issues. Can you imagine if I hadn't been observant? I eat a graham cracker and in eight hours I'm vomiting. With a freshly closed chest. The moral here, dear friend, is that you can never, ever let your guard down. The only advocate you always have is yourself. Erin had been a champ as my advocate all along. Now, however, she was waiting in the room, and I had to fend for myself. The technician threw away everything that had been prepared, sterilized the area, and started again with a celiac friendly test.

Or as they put it:

"Modified barium swallow was performed. The patient was given oral contrast of various consistencies by the speech pathologist and observed fluoroscopically swallowing in the lateral position.

"Tested consistencies included: Thin liquid by spoon and straw, puree by teaspoon, hard solids, and mixed consistency (thin liquids/hard solids)"

I told you I passed. They said:

"Laryngeal penetration occurred with: None of the tested consistencies.

"Aspiration occurred with: None tested consistencies.

"There was no significant residue following swallows.

"IMPRESSION:

"Normal modified barium swallow."

Seems like the same thing to me. Like the first time I did the test though, it was neat watching the glowing white stuff go down my throat. I was loaded back up and taken back to my room and to the waiting arms of my loving wife. Not her arms, exactly—she was working when I got back—but she did say hello.

I still wasn't hungry, but I was extremely thirsty. The doctor had compared me to a potato chip at this point. I was on some medicines to help dry me and my lungs out, and as a result, I was filling up that pee-pee bag pretty regularly. Now, though, I had passed my swallow test, so I could drink! I asked for a ginger ale. This was a mistake. Friends, if you ever find yourself in this situation, you should not ask for a ginger ale as your first drink in five days. It was a little too fizzy. I should've just asked for water. Not me, nooo. I decided to go all-in. While this was a small mistake, at least I was drinking again. The hope was that tomorrow solid foods would be allowed, and that maybe I'd want them.

Erin said goodbye. It was time for her to head home and see the girls. Thanks again to our friend, there was a meal waiting. The generosity of our friends and neighbors was amazing throughout. Today I even felt like FaceTiming the girls. It was great to see them and just hear them talk about their day. Sure, I had a few things to say, but it was about them and it was great. Too soon, it was time to say goodbye and try to get some rest. Ha! Rest in the ICU. Once again, I was alone with my thoughts. Good thoughts were winning out over negative ones now. The nurses had set my tray and phone up such that I could reach things without having to move too much. This meant I could get to my Switch and my phone whenever I wanted without calling them. I couldn't read at this point because of how foggy my mind was. Through the night, as I was in and out of rest and visitors came in and out, I played a few games and listened to music. Music is a great healer and it was working for me. There were several artists that really helped me. One song in particular was sort of a rally cry for me. "Get Better" has the lines:

I'm trying to get better because I haven't been my best

She took a plain black marker, started writing on my chest

She drew a line across the middle of my broken heart

And said, come on now, let's fix this mess

We could get better

Because we're not dead yet."

My heart was healing, my lungs on the mend. I had much to live for, and my recovery was proving that I had the mettle to see it through.

February 26

Things were getting hard. Not the healing, so much, just the *being*. I was exhausted. I was not resting and it was starting to show. It's one of the great ironies of being in the hospital. They tell you to rest and heal and then they aggravate the ever-loving shit out of you the entire time. Again, most people in the unit were not as alert and mobile as I was. In fact, I wasn't long for the ICU and would soon be moving to the step-down unit. Once I got to step-down, the next move was home. Erin was tired too. She had been driving back and forth, still being a care-giver, a wife, a mother, and full-time worker. Many people, including lots of her clients, assumed she took this time off from work. She did not. I don't know how she managed to do it all. It is a testament to how friggin' amazing she is. She was operating on a day-to-day basis but she was making it happen. She was making it happen, and while she said she was fine, her eyes were telling a different story.

As tired as I was, there were victories today. Yes, my day began with the three a.m. visit from the x-ray folks, and my morning routine was the same as the day before, but we made progress. The biggest thing for me was getting the central line removed from my neck. Since I was successful with the swallow test, I was allowed to take oral medications. This meant not only that I was losing the monstrosity that was connected to me, but that I was starting to take the medicines as I would after I got home. It also meant that I no longer resembled an electric car being charged. Best of all, it meant that I could finally turn my head! Sweet sassy-frassy, I could turn my head! Who knew there was something to my right and my left? The blinders were removed. Maybe all this would help me rest. Time would tell.

I doubled my walking from the day before as well: 600 feet—twice. I was getting good at leaving my room, turning right, and then making a bunch of lefts. I felt like I was in a race. A real slow race, but a race just the same. Not only was I walking, but I was talking while I did it. I'm not sure how much everyone else enjoyed me talking as I walked, but it felt good to me!

The only real line I had going in me at this point was the epidural. I still had the IV connection in my left arm as a "just in case" point of entry, but with the central line gone from my neck, that was all, and it was glorious. The decision was made to put a PICC line in my right arm. According to the Mayo Clinic:

> A peripherally inserted central catheter (PICC), also called a PICC line, is a long, thin tube that's inserted through a vein in your arm and passed through to the larger veins near your heart. Very rarely, the PICC line may be placed in your leg.

> A PICC line gives your doctor access to the large central veins near the heart. It's generally used to give medications or liquid nutrition. A PICC line can help avoid the pain of frequent needle sticks and reduce the risk of irritation to the smaller veins in your arms.

It's the last line there that was so key. Because I would still be getting frequent blood draws, and as time would have it, IV medicines again, getting rid of frequent needle sticks was great. The ladies showed up to put it in. I was their last patient of the day, and in fact, there was some concern that it might not happen today and I'd have to wait until the next day to get mine. But they made it, and I was glad they did. I can still see where the line went into my right arm. It's in my upper arm, just below my bicep. Essentially, they raised my bed, sterilized everything, and then inserted the catheter into my arm. They secured it and then left. That was it. It was awesome. Now, whenever there was a need for anything to enter or exit my veins, all that had to be done was to connect to the port and either take out or put in what was needed. No more needle sticks!

The only bummer for today was that I wasn't allowed to eat. One of the surgeons was still a bit wary of letting me eat as there seemed to be some residual barium left in my digestive tract. He wasn't altogether sure that my digestive system was fully awake and he didn't want there to be a traffic jam in my intestines. I was disappointed, but it was hard to argue with his logic. It's not like I was hungry; it just felt like a setback, though it really wasn't one. I kept pounding liquids just the same and kept flushing those kidneys. I had also managed to convince them that there was no need to continue finger sticks for glucose monitoring. An increase in blood sugars can occur post-transplant and some recipients have to go on insulin or have their sugars constantly monitored. My sugars had never even been elevated, so we could agree that there was no need to keep doing this.

There were highs and lows that day, and that would become the story moving forward. The big "sexy" was over. Now, the unsexy work was happening. It was easy to get caught up in the wonder of receiving new lungs. It is a wonder, to be sure. Another person's selfless act had given me another chance at life. It doesn't get any more glorious than that. What came next was up to me. How far would I walk each day? How hard would I press to eat, to bathe, to do anything? That was up to me. It wouldn't always be amazing and glory-filled, but it was required. Lots of things in life are like that. Sometimes we receive that big splash in life, and it's what we do after the spotlight fades that will determine how much the splash matters.

I had been in the hospital since Sunday, and the twenty-sixth was Friday. I had been in the ICU since the twenty-third. Three days. That was it. Three days, and so much had changed. I was making great progress. My time in the ICU was drawing to a close, that much was clear as we headed toward the weekend. Just like that, Erin went home and I started my nightly routine of trying to rest. I'm sure you're wondering if I rested that night.

Not much, honestly. I still wasn't ready to attack what was going on in my mind. My body was still healing, and I hadn't begun to address the amount of mental healing I was going to need. At this moment it was just too much. No doctor could help. My nurses were wonderful in this regard. They allowed me to just vent and talk it out. They didn't try to "fix" anything. They just listened. For all of the support I had throughout this entire process, this part of the journey was one that only I could take. No two paths through this were the same and I could only walk mine. I felt alone as I stared at these paths. That feeling of loneliness was one that would continue well into the future.

February 27

It's been said that the only thing they ain't making more of is land. They're forgetting one thing and perhaps the most important thing of all: time. Land is there, and we can buy it, in theory. No amount of money can buy you one more second on this planet. From the day we are born, the clock is ticking toward our end. It might be sooner rather than later. We just don't know. As I lay in the ICU that night, time became important to me. In 2018, we went on a weekend trip to Nashville to catch a Frank Turner concert. Luckily, we were also able to catch John Prine at the Ryman. I am really thankful we took advantage of the change to see him, since he would go on to become a victim of COVID. On that trip, we went to the Country Music Hall of Fame. They had a rotating exhibit with current trends in country music. It was fortunate for me that they had a display case featuring Jason Isbell. Jason is another one of those artists whose words speak to me. Another son of the South, he writes from a place many can only dream of. In this display were the handwritten lyrics to his song "If We Were Vampires." The song speaks to the preciousness of time and how it is a finite resource in our lives. One line in particular continues to resonate with me, so much so that I had it tattooed on my forearm in his handwriting even before this whole process started. That line is: "Maybe time running out is a gift." There that night, I felt that I had been gifted another chance at a little more time.

February 23, the day my surgery was complete, would be my re-birth-day. My time had run out on my old life. Now I had been given the gift of a reset. I was determined to make the most of it. I told you that I shouldn't be left alone with my thoughts. My head is a scary place. I was still very much focused on the physical healing ahead, and I thought I was beginning to address the mental side of things. Turns out, I was wrong. The mental side of things would become a recurring problem. I was dealing with the immediate impacts of a life-altering event. I was not dealing with how that would shape me moving forward.

February 27 was my last day in the ICU. It was determined by all of those wonderful doctors that I had progressed enough to be moved across the hall to the step-down unit. This was good news as it put me one step closer to home. Following the same morning routine of x-rays, move to chair, visits from doctors, Erin's arrival, etc. was becoming old hat. I spent a fair amount of time, as much as I could, walking. We have no definitive record of how far I walked on the twenty-seventh, but according to Erin it was a decent amount and with frequency. I was trying my best to get stronger.

A little known fact about getting new lungs: they have to inflate. Turns out, when they put them in, they aren't fully ready. It takes time for you to get full function out of them. There are a variety of factors that will impact just how much function you get. For some recipients, they may only get up to 80% function; some may reach 110%. The walking helps to inflate them, but the doctors also "gifted" me what would become the bane of my existence, an incentive spirometer. The device is made of a tube attached to a chamber with a float in it. I was to inhale as deeply as I could to get the float to rise as much as possible. There are markings along the outside of the chamber denoting how many milliliters of air I was inhaling. They set the target at 1500mL, and I was to place my mouth on the mouthpiece and inhale several times an hour. The nurses, the doctors, and Erin would enforce the use of this device. I hated it. It was necessary, but painful. Inhaling as deeply as they wanted was painful, due to having recently had my chest splayed open. I wasn't as diligent in using the device as I should've been, and that's on me. Only I could actually do the work. Taking in these deep breaths were stretching out my lungs and helping them to fill my pleural cavity. I was fortunate that my cavity had not shrunken too much through my disease. With some cases of ILD, the cavity shrinks with the lungs. This doesn't give the new lungs much room to grow. Since I got so sick so fast, this didn't happen. My lungs had room to grow. I had to exercise them.

I was able to start eating solid food as well. The problem was that nothing tasted good. My appetite still wasn't great, and the medicines were giving everything a bitter taste. Since it had been almost a week since my last solid food, the doctors really wanted to start getting some calories in me. Eating would be central in my recovery as I sought to regain strength and stamina. Erin tried everything. She gave me a Snickers—no dice. She gave me crackers—no go. Even my favorite homemade cookies, which Emma had made just before I went to the hospital, were not a hit. Butter crackers with crunchy peanut butter dipped in chocolate should have been awesome, but sadly they too were a miss. Eating would be a problem for the rest of my time in the hospital. Because of my celiac, the dietician had worked it out that I would preorder my meals with a set time for delivery. I spoke directly with management to place an order. The hard part was trying to decide what would be good the next day, or, since it was the weekend, the next two days. Many times, my food would arrive and I just couldn't eat it. It was a problem. I hear people in the pre-transplant phase talking about what they're going to eat in the hospital as soon as they can. It sounds neat, but no one really prepares you for the fact that, maybe, nothing will be good.

While I navigated my way through the day, we were just waiting for a room to open up in the step-down. The plan had been to move me today, but as the day wore on it was looking more and more like I'd spend one more night in the ICU. In fact, we had pretty much resigned ourselves to this when at around five thirty p.m., they came to tell me it was time to move. We gathered up what few things I had in the room, I got one last look at my great view, and I walked out of the ICU and across the hall to the step-down unit. That's right, I walked out of the ICU! I left a huge room with what could only be considered 24-hour concierge service to go to a room that was decidedly … not that.

My room in the step-down was in the corner of the unit. Upon entering the room, the conversation between me and the nurse went something like this:

"I'd like to speak with a manager please, these accommodations are not suitable."

"We're sorry sir, but this is the only room available."

"Well, this just won't do. Where am I to put all of my things? How am I to get get all of my bags and containers around the bed to reach the bathroom? What is that smell? Why am I sticking to the floor? Was this room last updated in the 1980s?"

"We know it's small and not the best, but we'll take really good care of you. Would you prefer to have the door to your room open or closed?" (as I hear the lady next door wailing)

"Closed please. Never leave that door open."

"You got it."

And thus began my time in step-down. I need to state straight away that the nurses were, for the most part, wonderful. But the room was shit.

It may have been that the room was in such a state as to encourage the rapid healing and discharge of patients. Once Erin had gotten me settled, she left. The look on her face was much like that of a parent leaving their kid at summer camp. She knew I was safe and I would be OK, but still …

7:00 p.m. and 7:00 a.m. were shift changes for nurses at the hospital, and I didn't get much chance to get to know the nurse that day as he was leaving pretty quickly. I liked him quite a bit though right off the top and would always enjoy it when he was assigned to me. The night nurse came on, introduced herself, and then did for the first time what would become the routine for the next week. Every night at seven, she'd come by with the day nurse, say hello, do a quick check of vitals, and move on to the next patient. She'd come back later to administer medicines and settle me in for the evening. In the step-down they only had to check on me every few hours, but I was still hooked up to all sorts of monitors and tubes, so there was lots to check on.

Then, she was gone, and I was again alone at night trying to figure all of this out. Now, though, I was in a much noisier and less restful environment. Leaving the television on would be the only way to pass the evenings. And at least it kept me out of my head. Sort of.

February 28

February had been quite the month for our little family. When the month began, I was more or less confined to bed and was dying. "End stage" was the wording, according to the notes in MyChart. We had weathered the storm of a dry run. We had experienced the highs of actually getting the call and excitement of being a "go." I had gone through the trauma of having my chest cut open and organs exchanged. I had been in ICU for less than a week. I was healing. I was still trying to figure all of this out. And now the month was over. I woke up my first morning in step-down excited to be out of the ICU and excited to look out of my window and greet the world. Instead of being greeted by a glorious sun-filled morning with blue skies and birds, I was greeted with the cold gray concrete of the exterior wall of the adjoining building with no view of the sky. Womp. Womp.

A bonus in step-down is that the x-ray folks don't come until four or so. An extra hour of not resting! Yay!! Other than that, the routine was the same: x-ray, recliner, doctors. Repeat. It was decided that I had drained enough fluid from my lungs to have two of my four chest tubes removed. This was quite a moment. More tubes coming out of my body! Here's how that process went:

Two doctors (fellows, to be exact) walked in.

"OK, Mr. Campbell, we're going to take out two of these chest tubes now."

"Sounds good to me."

"Here's what we're going to do. On the count of three I want you to take a deep breath, and then as you exhale, I need you to hum."

"Why do I hum?"

"Well, you hum so that air doesn't enter the hole and we can sew you up without creating any kind of extra air in there. We need it to stay out."

"I can do that."

"As you hum, I'll pull out the chest tube, and my associate will pinch together the skin. You can stop humming at that point. The surgeon went ahead and put a stitch in you during surgery, so all I have to do is tie the knot."

"Cool. Let's do it."

"One … two … three."

And just like that, the chest tubes came out. It didn't hurt; in fact, I barely felt it. Progress.

The doctors did decide to leave the epidural in one more day, and as a result, the catheter had to stay as well. Maybe tomorrow. Sadly, food was still not tasty, and rest was still challenging. That was Sunday in step-down.

March

March 1

Things were starting to progress and move along at a fairly rapid clip for me at this point, but there would still be highs and lows over the next few days for sure. All of these ups and downs would start to weigh heavily on my mental health and I was starting to get tired. I was tired of being where I was, tired of having to face this. It was a funny thing. I had been given the gift of a second chance, but I was pissed at the world. Some of the frustration was a function of being hungry and tired. I wasn't resting and I wasn't eating. I had absolutely no appetite. Food was still tasting bitter, and due to all the medicines I was taking, I was nauseated most of the time. These physical issues, added to the whole transplant thing, had me in a bad place. I was having difficulty feeling grateful for a second chance at life when I could only focus on being angry at my situation. And you know what? My feelings were completely valid. People would tell me that they had been praying and that God had delivered a miracle to me. I'm glad they felt that way. To me, I felt that if "God" were truly listening and praying truly worked, I would not be in this situation at all. They could get out of here with the whole, "God gives us only what we can handle" talk. I felt like I had been fighting for years, and I was getting tired. Now, however, the only way was forward.

March 2

A nd forward we pressed. On the first, I had one more chest tube removed. It was decided on the morning rounds, the ones that happened before sunrise, that one tube would come on out. The process was exactly the same as the day before; it was quick and it was over. That left me with only one remaining. Progress. The decision was also made to remove my epidural. When the doctor told me it would come out, he said I could expect to feel a fair amount of discomfort. I told him that I didn't think it would be that bad, as my pain had been pretty minimal. He said, "Yeah … Because of the epidural." Smart guy, that doctor.

In the late afternoon hours of the first, the pain management folks showed up to take out the epidural. Here's the thing. They should "pre-load" you with some type of pain relief. I don't necessarily mean an opiate, though that might have helped. Hell, I'd have been happy with Tylenol. That's not how they do things, though. I sat on the edge of the bed, and in one swift movement, the epidural was out. At precisely the same moment, a flood of pain entered my chest, and it felt as if it were on fire. Except for when the fentanyl was lowered, this was the only time in this whole process that I felt true pain. Just twice, that was it. Not prior to transplant, not any other time after, and not once I got home. This pain was a 10 on their stupid "1–10" pain scale. It was a burning like none I've ever experienced, and the poor nurse and PA would spend the next couple of hours trying to get the pain under control. They hit me pretty hard right off the bat with a cocktail of medicines to get the pain down. Their efforts were successful, and after about two hours, I was at least down to a five. It would come down some more, but woo boy. That was tough.

You want to know what else was tough? Getting a catheter removed. That also happened on the first. I tell you something, looking back on it now, the first was quite the day. When the doctor decided the epidural could come out, they also decided that the catheter could be removed. I was doing a great job of maintaining a good "fluid balance." It would be removed tonight, once the night nurse could get to it. It would be removed after the epidural came out, but what's a little more pain for one day? My night nurse tonight was wonderful and would be wonderful every time she worked, which was the majority of my time there. In fact, we got on so well she requested to be on my end of the hall. We just clicked, and she was an angel. After the initial rounds, she returned around eight and told me that she'd be back to take out the catheter around eleven p.m. Erin had long since left at this point, which left me alone to not eat and to ponder the upcoming removal of said catheter. I was told it would be important that I go to the bathroom soon after removal to prove that things were still working, or they might have to re-insert the thing. No pressure, Ronald. No pressure. There I lay, thinking about this upcoming adventure for three hours. Eleven p.m. arrived and Nurse Angel (not her real name, but what she will forever be to me) entered my room …

"OK, Ronald. It's time" (I never wanted the nurses to call me Mr. Campbell, or for anyone to call me that actually).

"Alright…"

Before I proceed with the details of the removal of said catheter, I feel a little bit of prelude is in order. I woke up from my surgery with the catheter already in place. I know, I know, but this is how it works. What I wasn't expecting was the amount of abuse the catheter and my little buddy would endure for the duration of its time nestled in there. Nurse's assistants would have to clean the catheter, which required a bit of pulling and tugging. I had one nurse in the step-down unit who treated my little buddy as if it were a tetherball. I'm not sure she needed to give it the attention she was, but she did. And it was not pleasant. Needless to say, by the time Nurse Angel was ready to remove the catheter, I was happy to oblige. After his week of abuse, though, my little buddy was a shell of his former self. At this point he resembled a turtle that had withdrawn into his shell. When Nurse Angel prepared him for removal, I was not all that excited to show him to her. He was not at his best, and I was a little embarrassed. I so badly wanted her to be in awe. She was not. I was sad. At least she had the professionalism to hold in her laughter. Back to the removal …

"Nurse Angel, how much is this going to hurt? Enquiring minds want to know," I asked.

"I've been told I do this pretty painlessly," she said.

"Tell, you what. You do what you need and I'll just look into your beautiful eyes as you do your business," I said. Of course, I was on medicines, so this was allowable.

"On three, I'm going to start to remove it. You ready?"

"I guess"

"One, two, three…"

And she pulled. She pulled the catheter for roughly 30 minutes (it was probably 10 seconds). It began to resemble the magic trick where the magician is pulling the handkerchief that never ends. When she finally reached the end of the catheter, there was one final tug, and POP, it was out.

"So, um. That hurt," I informed her.

"I am so sorry."

I couldn't stay mad at her. We had been through too much now, and she had seen things on me that she couldn't unsee.

"Well, now that you have seen that, I suppose there's no need for me to hold the gown closed when I get out of bed," I mentioned. She laughed.

"No, I guess not. Whenever you're ready, let me know, and we'll see if the plumbing is working."

Immediately, I told her that I wanted to go to the bathroom and see if I could get things flowing. I was successful in having a good little pee and this impressed her. She said she had never had a patient immediately go to the bathroom after having a catheter removed. At least I was able to impress her in some fashion on this night. I'll take what I can get.

I didn't sleep well after my fairly eventful day. It was more restful than some of my previous nights, but still not great. I was on medicines that were making my stomach shaky at best, and I typically like to sleep on my stomach. This was currently impossible; I was only on my back and pretty much unable to even rotate onto my side.

Mid-morning on the second, I started to wheeze. I heard it from the outset and it got so loud that Erin could hear it from across the room. It was loud. And it shook me a bit. Everything had been going so well for me that this unnerved me just a bit. The pulmonologist heard it when he made his rounds and decided that it was concerning enough that he wanted me to have a bronchoscope done. The surgeon who performed my surgery also heard it and concurred that a bronchoscope would be prudent. Neither one were concerned enough that the procedure was an emergency, but it still needed to be done. And it would happen the next day.

Other than the issue with the wheezing, the second was fairly uneventful. I was still not eating, mostly just drinking Ensures. To be completely honest, I was tired of them too. Their viscosity was challenging, but it was about the only thing I could get down. I wasn't walking nearly as much as they wanted. I was tired and starting to get hungry. I was also starting to smell myself. For the most part, the nurse's assistants were nice enough, but my interactions with them were primarily limited to them checking my vital signs. Whenever I'd ask to help get clean, there was always a "reason" why they "didn't have time, not right now…" I couldn't do it myself, and I was a little embarrassed by it all. Physical therapy had all but disappeared from my life. I was under the impression that they would be working with me to get my strength up and prepare me to go home, but by this point I had only seen them about once. I'd inquire about them and it was as if speaking into the ether. I was one week post-transplant at this juncture and starting to go a little crazy. Nurse Angel was off tonight, so I had to live with another nurse. A good one, certainly, but not mine.

My head and body were tired. The world outside was still spinning and people were doing more and more. Probably one of the worst things I had access to while in the hospital was social media. I could see what everyone was doing, and it reminded me of what I wasn't doing. I so badly wanted to get back out there and start living again, but so much work lay ahead of me. And it would be work that I would have to put in without fanfare. People would try to tell me that I was lucky and that I should be grateful for the second chance. True statements, sure. The thing is, though, I didn't ask for any of this crap. I was trying to make sense of the unfairness of being in this situation at all and the gratefulness of another chance. To the best of my knowledge, I had done nothing in my life to bring this disease on me. I guess it really didn't matter anymore. I've said it before: things just happen. How we deal with them shows who we are. As I was in bed that night, I was still feeling very alone. The world was indeed going on without me, and that included my family. Was the fight worth it?

March 7

The scope didn't actually happen till later on in the day, so I spent most of the day following the same routine as the previous week. X-rays, vitals, move to the recliner, doctor visits, Erin arrives, more visits, medicines, etc., etc., etc. We were settling in to a routine, but it was one that I was growing weary of. There had been talk of sending me home on Thursday the fourth, and I had not been comfortable leaving quite that soon. Fortunately, my wheeze prevented it from happening, and now the target date was Monday the eighth. The physical therapy team actually showed up the morning of the seventh to walk me and start checking things off to release me. The issue was that I was not, at that point, in a position to go walk. I was dealing with the steady stream of doctors, and I asked the physical therapist to come back around two as my scope was scheduled for three-ish. The wheezing was gone by now, having corrected itself when I coughed up a good bit of "secretions," but we would do the scope just the same.

The physical therapist never showed. Of course he didn't. The transport folks did show up and put me in a bed to go down to surgery to have the scope done. As I was in the bed and starting the move, the therapist showed up.

"Ready to go walk?" he said.

"Seriously, dude? I'm in a bed being transported to surgery. Where were you an hour ago?" came my reply.

"Oh, uh, I'm sorry. I guess time got away from me."

"We're gonna need to reschedule."

You might remember that I mentioned my desire to have my door closed. My next-door neighbor was a screamer. Everything that was done to her caused her to wail in pain, and when she wasn't wailing in pain, she was talking loudly on the phone, often around two a.m. As I was waiting to be transported downstairs for my bronchoscope, she was being discharged. Thankfully. However, she wasn't going quietly. She had decided that she needed to take everything from her room that wasn't secured to the floor or walls. This lady had packed up absolutely everything in her room and was trying to abscond with the whole thing. As I lay in my bed for transport, I heard the nurses and transport guy trying to calmly tell her that no, she could not take everything with her. Her rationale was that she knew how they nickeled and dimed everyone in the hospital, so she was going to take what she wanted to make up for that. The nurses calmly explained that that was not how it worked, and unless she relented, they would be forced to call security. She decided that being discharged without linens was better than dealing with security. All of this happened while I was lying there just waiting to go downstairs. It did bring a touch of levity to my day, and it provided a bit of comic relief for the rest of my time in step-down.

Despite this little sideshow, my patience was wearing thin. With the whole damn thing. I got to the surgery room, where the surgeon was waiting for me. I was put under anesthesia again, and they sent a scope down my nose and into my lungs to have a look around, then took a small sample to biopsy to check for fungal growth and cellular rejection. The surgeon was happy to report to Erin that everything was great and that the lungs were in amazing shape.

Slowly, I emerged from the fog of anesthesia back in my room and saw Erin. She reported the results to me, and we both had a sigh of relief. I did wake up with a new tube. The surgeon had decided to put in a wound vacuum in order to help my chest drain a bit faster. Essentially, this was a tube with a sponge on the end, secured to my chest with a bandage creating an airtight seal. Every now and then, the vacuum would kick on and keep the suction going. It wasn't a big deal, but it meant I wouldn't be able to go home until the doctors were satisfied with the drainage and that my cavity was "dry."

That bronchoscope was the last procedure I would face in the hospital. For the rest of my time there, I fell into a pattern. My iron levels and magnesium levels were low, and as a result, I had to receive infusions of both through my PICC line. It wasn't a big deal, just very time consuming. The iron took about two hours, the magnesium a little longer, and I had to do it at least twice a day, occasionally three times. I'd begin the first one early in the morning, have a small break, do one in the afternoon, and then end my day with the last one, finishing up around eleven p.m. That meant that from roughly five a.m. to eleven p.m., I was hooked up to an infusion. If I went anywhere—the bathroom, for a walk, anywhere—I was dragging that darned IV stand with me. It made navigating tricky.

On top of that, the medicines were messing with my mind. I was starting to have hallucinations. I had been told that this was normal, but boy, let me tell you, it was something else. I can understand why some people gravitate toward drugs. I saw and felt things that were out of this world. Once, the walls were flowing with water. One time, I asked Erin why our dog was beside me. Those were the tame ones. Between the medicines and getting stir crazy, I was out of my mind. I could even time out how fast I'd feel the effects. When the effects kicked in, I couldn't follow anything. Erin was able to spend her time working as I rambled on aimlessly.

On Thursday of that week, the social worker stopped by to check on us. The nurse coordinator stopped by to schedule our "So, You're Going Home" talk, and we set up a talk with the nutritionist about what to do upon discharge. Clearly things were moving in that direction. Until then, everything depended on me maintaining the same level of progress, getting out the wound vacuum, and clearing physical/occupational therapy.

Remember how I've said I had a steady rotation of the door opening and closing with all kinds of people coming and going? Remember how I said it was impossible to rest with all this? It was refreshing when the nutritionist got to experience this first hand. All through her discussion, she was constantly interrupted, to the point where she lost her mind.

"How do you deal with this?!?" she asked.

"You don't. I'm so tired of it. Y'all want me to rest and heal, but this is how my day goes. And my night."

It was nice that someone from the team finally had to experience a small part of my struggle. As wonderful as the team was and continues to be, they were not living the daily struggle. I'm not trying to minimize their work, but ultimately, they could return home. Looking back, I suppose all of this was meant to allow me the chance to do the same.

The pharmacist also met with us to start getting everything lined up for the medicines I would take home with me. There would be some need to talk to an outside pharmacy, but most of my prescriptions could be filled at the hospital. All of them would be delivered to my house. Sweet.

And so the days ticked by. Slowly. Very slowly. My nurses and I developed a good relationship. I was their least needy patient and they started to leave me alone. My day nurse even put a sign on my door for folks to not bother me for certain times so I could get some friggin' rest. My night nurse got used to me unhooking from the monitors so I could go to the bathroom. With each visit, I let them know that I had left them some pee to measure because my fluid was still being closely monitored. I did have the occasional breathing treatment that required everyone to leave my room for 30 minutes or so, and I was still being forced to use that incentive spirometer. All in all, it wasn't terrible. It was just boring. I was ready to go and starting to get agitated about my confinement.

On Saturday the sixth, I had my first visitor other than Erin. My mom came to spend the day. It was a pleasant change of pace from the other days, it was nice to see her, and it was good for Erin to have a break. She also made sure that I received some of the things I had been missing. She made the nurses change my sheets; she made them get me a clean gown; she had them get me things to clean up. She also saw how useless the nurse's assistants were. I was glad to have her there for the day. Erin didn't quite get the day off, though. She and Emma had to go to Greenville for accepted students' day at East Carolina. They called me on the way home to regale me with tales of their day. It was great to hear the excitement in Emma's voice as she talked about everything. Her excitement spilled over and reminded me why I was fighting. I was fighting to be a part of my kids' lives for as long as possible. It was a much needed reminder.

Nevertheless, by the time Erin returned on Sunday, I was in a foul mood. I was done. I was done with being in the hospital. Done with being hooked up and monitored. Done with the steady stream of folks. Done with medications. Done with infusions. Done with being gone. Done. The medicines were still making me weird, and I was convinced that someone was trying to attack me. My frustration was misplaced, and I was too brusque with Erin. She had been nothing but awesome throughout this whole process, and I felt bad. She asked the nurse if she could put me in a wheelchair and take me on an excursion just to get me off the floor. I hadn't seen the sky since the twenty-first of February. She was told no. It was frustrating.

On Sunday, in between all of the infusions, the wound vacuum came off. For the first time since I went on oxygen at night back in August, I was free and untethered. When I wasn't receiving an infusion I had no tubes or wires. I felt like Pinocchio becoming a real boy, with no strings to tie me down. I convinced my nurse to walk with me to the stairwell so I could demonstrate that I could use steps. Since this was something I had to "pass" to leave, and since no physical therapist seemed intent on coming by, I wanted her to see it and to note it in my chart. I was tube-free and walking. I was becoming human again. I still wasn't eating all that much, but when I did eat, food was beginning to taste better. I told them that if they'd just let me go home,

I'd heal right on up. I demonstrated to the occupational therapist my ability to perform functions of daily living that day as well. I showed her I could bathe (sort of), deal with personal hygiene, and dress myself. All of the boxes were checked. The doctors were satisfied. Barring any issues overnight, my discharge would be on Monday the eighth.

My progress had been remarkable. We were told to expect a three-to-four-week stay in the hospital. I was out of the hospital 13 days after receiving new lungs. It was amazing. It was due to my efforts, but also to the efforts of an amazing staff of medical professionals, and to the care Erin showed. No man is an island.

On the eighth, we started the process of getting me outta there. There were final visits from the doctors for last checks, the nurses came to say goodbye, and other members of the transplant team stopped in for farewells. The last piece of the puzzle was waiting for the pharmacist to bring me my medicines. He arrived, went over them, we placed them in a large pill box, and that was that. I was sent home with the following medicines (though they would change):

- Prograf (tacrolimus), .5mg. Antirejection
- Cellcept (mycophenolate mofetil), 500mg. Antirejection
- Prednisone, 5mg. Anti-rejection
- Valcyte (valganciclovir hydrochloride), 450mg. Prevents CMV infections
- Noxafil (posaconazole), 100mg. Prevents and treats fungal infections
- Zithromax (azithromycin), 250mg. Prevents and treats bacterial infections and chronic rejection
- Calcium, 600mg
- Magnesium oxide, 400mg
- Amlodipine besylate, 5mg. Controls blood pressure

- Aspirin, 81mg. Prevents blood clots

- Pravachol (pravastatin sodium), 20mg. Lowers cholesterol

- Bactrim (sulfamethoxazole/trimethoprim), 400mg/80mg. Prevents and treats bacterial infections

- Fosamax (alendronate sodium), 70mg. Prevents and treats osteoporosis

I was also sent home with some gabapentin, Tylenol, and anti-anxiety pills. Other than the Tylenol, I stopped those fairly quickly. It would be up to me to fill the pill box weekly and keep a watchful eye on taking the medicines exactly as prescribed, with zero flexibility. The doctors were quite adamant about that. Some of the pills I would only take once a day, though most were twice daily. With the new medicines, there were also new dietary restrictions in place. This was going to be challenging. I was instructed that I had to monitor my blood pressure, temperature, weight, and pulse in a journal, and if there were issues, I had to contract the clinic. No problem. Let me go. Now, please.

I had already dressed. Erin had packed the room up (there wasn't much). And we departed. There was no fanfare, no band, no clapping. I just … left. I honestly felt that it was a bit anti-climactic. Here I had fought through so much, and I as I left, I was already a memory to those in the unit. The medical transport wheeled me out of the step-down and down to the valet pick-up. Memories of pre-transplant visits for testing and clinic visits came flooding back. Erin got me in backseat of the car and we set off for home. It was a painful ride home. My chest was sore and my incision was in a delicate state. I felt each and every bump on the way home, and by the time we pulled in the driveway, I was exhausted.

But then … Then I saw my girls. For the first time since the twenty-first, we were all in the same place together. When I left them for the hospital, I wasn't sure I'd see them again. Now, in less than two weeks, in my driveway

I was getting a hug from my daughters and seeing my dog's wagging tail. As happy as I was, all I wanted to do was get upstairs and lay down in my bed.

Rachel brought me a cane. I used it to get in the house, but I wouldn't use it for long. I took a short break, then I went upstairs. I had been told to stay downstairs for the first day or two I was home by the physical therapist. She didn't want me using stairs initially, and once I did, she wanted me to take them one at a time. One step, two feet. Step up. Two feet on the tread. Screw that. I followed the directions of the therapist and did the stairs gingerly, but I did not stay downstairs and I would not use her method long. The way I figured it, the only way to get stronger and get better faster was to push. If I acted like I was sickly, I'd stay weaker longer, and I didn't have time for that. Senior night was fast approaching. We got my bed set up to where I was more or less comfortable. It wasn't perfect, but I was home. Holy shit. I was home. Now the work began.

Post-Hospital

We marked time in the hospital in days. Once I got home, we started to be able to mark it in weeks. I went home on a Monday. The first thing that I had to do would be on Thursday of that week, March 11. I would learn early on that there was no time off when rehabbing from a lung transplant. The great benefit was that I was at least able to rest, even if I wasn't sleeping well. I would need to adjust to life at home, but not having the constant interruptions was glorious. I was slowly reintroducing foods into my life and the first thing that actually tasted good was a microwave macaroni and cheese. Don't judge me. It was good and I ate all of it. I was a big boy. Anyway, that Thursday I had to go to pulmonary rehab back in Chapel Hill. I would have to go three times a week until I was able to meet their benchmarks. Erin had set me up with rides with her uncle, her dad, and my dad. We were trying to share the load. People had been wanting to help, and this was a tangible thing they could do.

First up to drive me was Erin's uncle. He showed up, and I used the cane to get out to his car. Again the ride wasn't great; I felt every bump between Raleigh and Chapel Hill. Upon arrival at rehab, I slowly made my way in using the cane. At this appointment, we were out to set some baselines for measurement. My legs were weak, which the therapist noted, and my stamina poor. All in all, I was there, but far from where I wanted to be. The therapist created a plan that I would follow in rehab and told me that the effort I put in at home would go a long way in my success. On Friday I made my first post-transplant visit to clinic, and everything was just peachy. There was a little fluid in my lung, so they had that removed. Essentially, they tapped my back, put a tube in, and syphoned out about 350mL of fluid. It wasn't a concern. The fluid showed no evidence of anything nefarious. It was just some buildup leftover from my stay in the hospital. I reminded myself that by all rights, I should have still been in the hospital with chest tubes, so this didn't bother me too much.

The next week I had three rehab trips. It was challenging to have so many, especially three days in a row. I hadn't done this much work in months. I continued to do well with my rehab, consistently making the therapist happy with my motivation and progress. The only way I was going to get better and back to normal was to do the work. And that is just what I was going to do. I had already gotten to the point where I had ditched the cane and was taking the stairs in a more normal way. Monday and Tuesday were big leg and stamina days. Apparently, actively dying for several months really drags down your muscle tone. But I saw a really big improvement in my leg strength this week. Wednesday was supposed to be another leg day, but the therapist decided to do some soft tissue massage and stretching with my incision area instead. I'm glad she did this. These stretches have been great at home.

My second week out I had another visit to the clinic. It was explained prior to discharge that I would go to clinic every Friday for the first month. This Friday's visit was good. All of my labs and x-rays looked good. There was no additional fluid build-up in my lungs, and my chest tube sutures were removed. The doctor also explained a bit why my chest was so tight. It turned out that as my old lungs were shrinking and dying, the pleural space was shrinking and filling with other stuff. Now that I had new lungs, the lungs were working to stretch out the space again. It would get better. It was yet another sign that I was healing.

It was becoming clear to me I was still doing a ton of physical healing. I was slowly becoming more able to sleep on my side. Sleeping on my stomach was still a no-go. And I still wasn't ready to start the mental healing yet.

From the time I got the call on the twenty-first to go in for my transplant, the date of March 26 had loomed large: senior night for the band.

This usually occurred in the fall, but this had not been a normal year. I was determined that I would be at Emma's senior night. I couldn't miss it. But would I be able to make it? I would have to get in the stadium, up some stairs, and sit through the first half. Then I'd have to walk the track, stand a bit, and then eventually cross the field with her. Would I have the strength and stamina to do this? Hell, I had just been in the hospital. I had only ditched the cane a week before. I didn't know if I'd make it, but just knowing it was coming was all the motivation I needed to work my ass off to get stronger. I would also have to do it after an early start that day, since I had to be at clinic at 7:30 a.m.

I had been working hard to meet goals in rehab. There was nobody to make me do the work. The therapist could only encourage me. I had to actually do it. It came down to heart and effort. Did I have it in me to do what I needed? In short, yes. On Tuesday the twenty-third, I celebrated the one-month anniversary of my transplant by going back to physical therapy. One month already. At rehab my progress would be evaluated. I celebrated by clearing another rehab goal (20 chair sit/stands in 30 seconds) and setting the target date of April 6 to be done with rehab altogether. On Wednesday, I walked a mile in 19 minutes. My post-transplant goal was a mile in 30 minutes. So, essentially, I met my 10-week goals in two weeks. It's not that I didn't like the ladies at rehab, I just had other things to do. I was proving to be the kind of patient they didn't often come across. I was motivated. I was strong. I was determined. I was tired of going to rehab so much.

At clinic everything was just great. My diagnostics were all good, good enough that they moved my visits from weekly to every two weeks. I also had my first post-transplant PFT (pulmonary function test). In a nutshell, my lungs were now operating at nearly triple where they were before surgery—and that would only improve. I was also able to walk into and around the hospital for the first time ever. No more wheelchairs for me. I ran into one of my nurses from the step-down unit. The surprise on her face was a look I've since gotten accustomed to. She was shocked at my progress. Some might call me a medical marvel. You know what? Feel free. I was truly bucking all of the trends. I think that so many transplant recipients are older that folks in clinic and rehab are not used to a somewhat young person who is ready to get on living.

Back to senior night. I made it. There was no way I wasn't going to walk with Emma. The year hadn't gone the way she had hoped. As frustrating as it was for her, it was frustrating for us as parents. This was not the way we wanted her to close out high school. When you have kids you imagine certain events certain ways. One thing that I was clobbered over the head with this year was that things often don't go the way we want. The crowd at the game was basically parents and siblings of seniors on the various teams, so it wasn't the great celebration that we had hoped. But at the end of the day, Erin was on one side, I on the other, and Emma in between us. With Rachel watching from the stands, it didn't matter who else was there. Our little family was there, and being together, when just a month ago everything was in flux, was all that mattered. As my physical healing started to morph into more mental healing, coming to recognize these small victories would be crucial.

This had been a hard month for everyone. I think for most everyone else, they felt the hard part was over. I was physically on the mend and no longer dying. And while this was true and important, the hard part for me was just starting. I was in a place that no one could relate to. There was nobody in my life who could understand what I was dealing with either physically or emotionally. I had lots to work through mentally, and that would be as hard as trying not to die. In many ways, it would be my biggest and most consistent challenge.

Life was clipping right along.

April

As another month began, I continued my routine of rehab and clinic visits and trying to find ways to occupy my time. Physically, I was healing right on up at a speed that defied all logic. I was putting in the work at home as well as at rehab and was way ahead of schedule. I was so far ahead of where most people were that everyone was forgetting how recent my transplant had been. It was getting hard being so limited in my freedom, especially since I felt like I should be allowed to do more. As one of my doctors told me, they were working for the long term. While I too was focused on living for many more years, I was ready to do stuff now. On Thursday the first, I received my first COVID vaccine. I went to the local Walgreens and got the Moderna shot. There are lots of questions over the efficacy of the vaccine on folks with solid organ transplants. I was told that a Johns Hopkins study was showing no real antibodies in transplant patients after the first shot. So, yay.

After my shot, we had to go back to the hospital for my donor-specific antibody (DSA) blood draw. Yep, a trip to Chapel Hill for one blood draw. It was a fairly important one, though. It detected whether or not my body was developing antibodies to my lungs, which could lead to rejection. I'm happy to tell you all that at my clinic appointment, they told me that everything there was negative. My body still liked my new lungs.

The first full week in April was a big one. On Monday, I had Emma and Rachel take me to a book shop. It was my first real excursion in months. And it was glorious. After we did that, Emma got her first COVID shot. We were on our way! On Tuesday, I went to physical therapy one more time, and I graduated. I completed my last task of walking a mile in 30 minutes (I walked it in less than 20). All of my future appointments except one were canceled! At the one remaining appointment the therapist would show Erin how to do some type of massage to help keep my incision from developing internal scarring. On Thursday both girls were able to finally attend school in person and feel kind of normal again. And, as a shout out to Rachel: her soccer team picked up two wins that week.

On Friday, I went to the clinic and received more good news. My labs, x-rays, and PFTs were all great. I was still showing increased lung function, and all the doctors, nurse practitioners, and pharmacists were happy. All in all, things were going great. I continued to heal, and my sternum and chest were not quite as sore. I'd even been able to lie on my stomach some, though sneezing was still an excruciating exercise. At this point, some of my biggest challenges were mental. I was doing all the physical things I needed to do. Where I was struggling was in my head. Right now, I was trying to figure out what part of "old me" was still there, and what the "new me" was going to be. I knew I had time to figure that out, but it was a struggle. But—I'd been given the gift of time. I could work through all of this.

All of this continues to be a mind-warp, and I look forward to the day when it's just *a* thing, and not *the* thing, that defines me. I look forward to the day when this whole saga is just part of my story.

———

While it looked like April was going great, the good news was not destined to last. Life is a series of random events with no real discernible pattern. There is no way to predict how things will go and no way to control any of it. The best that you can do (other than fall in love, when caught between the moon and New York City) is take each day as it comes and make it to the next, trusting that things can and will improve.

From a health standpoint, I was doing well. I did have some slightly lowered tacrolimus levels last week. They wanted me at 9, and I was at 8.5. This medicine was one of my anti-rejection medicines, so it was fairly critical that its levels were right. They decided to add one more pill to my evening dose and check it the following week. I continued my rehab at home by walking every day, sometimes twice, and lifting five-pound weights. On Thursday, I went to have my tac level checked. This time is was at 13.5—so a bit elevated. My creatinine levels (kidney stuff) were good, so they left the dosage the same and decided to see what it would be at clinic on the twenty-third. I went to the PT clinic for the therapist to show Erin how to do deep tissue massage on my chest and scar to keep things loose. I was excited about the prospect of two ladies rubbing on my chest at the same time. I should not have been excited. It hurt. Like, really hurt. I woke up Friday bruised in a couple of spots, and sore.

The real challenges for our family would come from other places. The week began innocently enough. The girls were back in school, soccer was happening, and everything was more or less normal. Then we got to Wednesday, and I was told by my doctors that I would not be able to go on the vacation we had scheduled to St. John, US Virgin Islands. They did not want me that far from a hospital, in case something happened. I spent that entire morning canceling the vacation that had, in all honesty, helped with my recovery. Last year, we had lost our trip to Italy because of COVID, this year was this year, and now we had lost St. John. I canceled rooms in St. Thomas, our killer villa, our jeep rental, and the flights. Each cancellation was like a kick in the pants. Intellectually, I got it. That did not make it easier. It's also hard when you make the mistake of looking at any social media and see people returning to normal and getting out there. We couldn't and that sucked. Long term, it'd be fine. Today, it was not. And don't say, "Well at least you're alive." While that's true, it's a fairly low bar when one is only 44. If this family didn't get a vacation, it might soon reach a critical point.

As if that wasn't enough for Wednesday, we got a call from the health department at three thirty informing us that Rachel had had a close contact with a COVID-positive student and would thus have to quarantine through the twenty-sixth. She' been in class for four days since they went back and now would miss 10 school days. Through no fault of her own. I spent the majority of the rest of the week contacting administrators, board members, central office staff, and anyone else we could think of. WCPSS seemed to be picking and choosing how to enforce COVID guidelines, allowing kids three feet of separation, but 14 days of quarantine (exceeding CDC guidelines) for all kids within six feet. It seemed that if Rachel tested negative today, seven days post exposure, she should be back in school Monday. Board policy was bad and there was no recourse for parents or students. This, too, sucked. Long term, it'd be fine. Today, it was not.

Additionally, this was the week of April 15, and while personal tax returns weren't due until May, all other returns—including estimates—were due on Thursday. Erin had been working hard, both at her job and to keep the family functioning. She was not sleeping well and needed a vacation more than anyone. Physically, I was healing right on up. Mentally, I was going stir-crazy, and all of us were stressed. Our lives this week had been impacted by things outside of our control and with little we could do to resolve them. But each new week brought fresh hope, and all I could do was try to be a positive voice and trust that things could improve. They had to.

As April came to a close, I had one more visit to clinic, and again everything was just fine. In the final week of the month, Rachel completed her school-imposed exile and was allowed back in the classroom. She never once had a positive test. Rachel had had more COVID tests than anyone in our house; I felt bad for her. At least she was back in school and on the soccer pitch for her final two games of the season. Because I had progressed so far, it was no issue for me to actually attend the last two games. Heck, she finally got to play on her home field for the first time this year. She was in the concussion protocol to begin the season, played an away game or two, then had her quarantine. She played well, though she didn't play much. There were tears in the car. She felt that she had disappointed me by not getting in the game. I had to remind her that, just like in life, it's not the amount of time that we get, it's how we use the time we're given. She might not have played much, but she really maximized her time. In the final game of the season at Enloe, she started and had an assist on the first goal of the game. I was so happy to have been able to be present for this first for her. She played a great game. Another lesson here for her. You have to put the disappointments of the day before in the rear view mirror. It's gone. Can't change it. But what you can do is make the most of the opportunity of today. It had been a hard month for our little clan. There were many highs. There were incredible lows.

As we navigated through each up and down, we sought to control as much as we could. It was evident to me how much was out of our hands. For so long now, I had been dealing with so many things that I simply could not do anything about. All I could do was focus on what I could control, however little that might be. Some days the only thing I could control was my sock choice. Some days the only thing I could control was my attitude. With Rachel's COVID exile, I couldn't control school policy, but I could work to get her access to what she needed to be successful. Like I told the principal, I was his worst nightmare. I was a smart dad with nothing else to do but annoy him until my daughter was taken care of. We all seek control. Sometimes that might be in our personal relationships, sometimes it's in the world at large. The only thing we can control is ourselves. Our effort, our attitude, our desire—that's it.

It helped that I was starting to venture back out into the world, even if only a little bit. I had gone to the bookstore with Emma and Rachel earlier in the month, true. Now, on the final Wednesday of the month, I went to dinner with Erin and our best friends. In an actual restaurant! It was glorious. We sat outside on a perfect evening and enjoyed great food and fabulous company. And you know what made the night better? We followed dinner up with a seated, socially-distant concert by the local band American Aquarium. I felt alive—finally. It was a small return to normal that had a huge impact on my attitude. Learning to live again was proving harder than I imagined, but we had taken all the challenges the month threw at us in stride. There were tears, there was sadness, but finally, this week had brought us a little joy as well.

May

M ay would be a big month for me. At the end of the month, I would find out if I had been cleared to finally join Erin in the front seat of the car, maybe drive, and be cleared to travel. There would be a lot riding on that clinic visit, but first we had to navigate the rest of the month. I couldn't look too far down the road. I needed to stay focused on the curve in front of me.

It was exciting that by mid-May, the girls had completed two weeks of actual school on campus. Well, sorta. They were there on campus until the great toilet paper, er, gas shortage of 2021 caused Wake County to move classes online for Friday the fourteenth. There was a "gas shortage" here on the East Coast after a gas pipeline was hacked and had to be shut down. As the week progressed, gas started to be harder to find. Just like the toilet paper issue the previous spring, this issue was caused by hysteria. If people had just remained calm … Oh well, one thing this whole transplant process had taught me was to try not to sweat things I couldn't control. Damn, there's that word again: control. The first part of the first week of May was a normal as possible around here. School, Erin working and trying to stay sane as tax season 2019—I mean 2020—I mean whatever the heck year—was coming to a close, and I was healing. I'd been walking two or three times a day around the neighborhood and doing my five-pound weights. Five pounds—I was ripped. All I needed now was a snazzy track suit and I could join up with the Mall Walkers.

Erin and I went to clinic on Friday the seventh, and everything there was just hunky dory. My labs were as expected, my x-rays boringly normal, and my evaluation ho-hum. The only real things of note were my PFTs. I need to brag here for just a second. At my sickest, just before transplant, I was in the low 20s for lung function. On the seventh, I hit 97%! This was better than expected. I almost floated out of that room. It had been suggested early on that I might hit 90% as my best result, but here I was at 97%. Yet again I was defying the odds and proving what a medical marvel I was. The only bummer was that I still wasn't cleared to drive or even sit up front. This meant that once we got back to the car, I was yet again imprisoned in the back seat. I really was getting sick of sitting there, but again, what could I do? My hope was that at my next clinic visit, I'd get the all clear.

Because everyone in the family was vaccinated, we were able to actually get together with our families for Mother's Day. If you had told me in early February that I'd be sitting there having a nice Mother's Day get-together with my mom, I wouldn't have believed you. Not because of her, but because I would have thought I would be dead. The being alive made it one of the more fun visits we'd had in a while, topped off by the banana pudding that Rachel had made and that was honestly the best one I've ever had. It's also the first one I'd had in over eight years, but it was phenomenal. On Sunday, we gathered with Erin's family for a pleasant visit. We were taking back our lives with slow, small, very tentative steps. On the Thursday after Mother's Day, my dad came up and took me to UNC, to the basement of the main hospital for some sort of routine testing on my GI system.

This was by far the most frustrating part of the process to date. From scheduling the appointment, to knowing where to go, to pre- and post-procedure instructions, it was a disaster. However, if this was to be my greatest aggravation, I'd take it.

We get to the hospital and I am taken back to a room. There the nurse talks to me a bit and I get into a shouting match with some disembodied phone voice. Because my chart showed very little as it related to this appointment, the nurse asked the voice to resend some information, and the voice balked. There was an exchange of ideas from me to her, and she wanted to argue with me about what I was and wasn't seeing in MyChart. Just send the stupid information!

My blood was boiling. Combine this with the overall frustration I had had from the start, and I was now in a mood. Then I had a pencil-thick catheter stuck down my nose into my esophagus and down into my stomach.

This test was to measure the effectiveness of my esophagus and make sure that peristalsis was occurring. It was. I coulda told 'em that. With all of this normal, the tube was pulled out, and a smaller-diameter catheter was placed in the same way and left for 24 hours to monitor my stomach acids. Here's a funny quirk that happened: I was told they needed 20 hours of good data to get an accurate reading. OK, but I wasn't supposed to eat after midnight to prep for the test the next day. That was in 12 hours. Good planning guys, good planning. I understood the pulmonologists wanting to make sure there was no reflux leading to potential aspiration into my new lungs. Reflux was one of the things that could lead to potential rejection. I wanted to make sure everything was cool too, but this whole process was just aggravating. With this catheter taped to my face for the fare-you-well, we left. I was in a very foul mood. I returned the next day to the hospital to have the tube removed (a visit I was unaware of until the previous day) and then returned to Meadowmont (the site of my first specialist visit) to have an upper GI done. I hadn't eaten since midnight, and my procedure was scheduled for 2:00 p.m. Grrr. No food, not much sleep, and prednisone. I was struggling to keep it together. This procedure was also to make sure there were no acid issues, and that my stomach, upper small intestine, esophagus looked good. They did. I coulda told 'em that.

As that week ended, I was getting better, but I was ready to be set free. I still don't think the doctors were used to dealing with young, motivated, active patients. I heard a recipient say recently that he was just grateful for one more day. I get it. I was grateful too, but I was ready to get on living. Having another day wasn't much use if I was constrained to my house and to some radius of the hospital. Get busy living or get busy dying, right? I was passing my days reading, playing my guitars (and actually improving), and trying to be a little more help around the house. There was still so much I couldn't do, but I could fold laundry and cook again. Getting back in the kitchen was great. It had been therapeutic, and dare I say, fun.

Earlier in the month, I had seen a chance for a bourbon tasting on the UNC Alumni page. Alcohol was one of those things that were on the no-fly list for me right now, and bourbon was already on there because of my celiac. I asked Erin if she wanted to do it and she jumped at the chance. Our good friend joined her. The bourbons arrived on our front porch, and I set up quite the spread and let them go. It was a great diversion for her, and it sounded like she had a great time. They were in our dining room, so I could actually hear the fun they were having. After the few months she had lived through, this little diversion was much needed. I was glad that my health was now in a state where she felt like she could let her hair down a little, even if only for one evening.

May flew by in the blink of an eye. Only having to go to clinic every two weeks was nice, but because of the other procedures, it wasn't the break I had hoped for. We thought it would be great, yet there we were in Chapel Hill all the time. There was a clinic visit on the seventh, then the GI stuff the next week, then another clinic trip on the twenty-first. Ah, but the twenty-first... Would I be cleared to drive? All of my labs, x-rays, and evaluations were fine. My PFT showed a slight decrease in function, so slight that it was within the margin of error for the machine. The technician wasn't in the least concerned; the pulmonologist thought it might be prudent to do a bronchoscope. I knew that my numbers couldn't keep going up forever, but having to do another scope felt like a kick in the pants. On the bright side, I was cleared to ride up front and drive! I couldn't wait to get to the car and actually see the world through the front windshield for the first time since February 21. It had been three months. It was hard to believe, but it was true. Some days, it felt as if the transplant had happened the day before. Some days it felt like years ago. This was a big day. Riding in the front seat on the way home was weird and unnerving, but exhilarating.

Not only was the twenty-first a big day from a clinical standpoint, it was a big day for the family too. Emma had her final band concert of her high school career, and Rachel had her first. The band director combined the concert and band banquet into one event. And I was there. I had come to believe that my presence was what mattered. Because of someone else, I had been given the chance at more time and could watch my daughters perform. Rachel was even awarded the Most Improved Member of her band, and Emma (along with the whole senior class) was awarded the "Overcoming" award. And. I. Was. There. I got to see it all. I was exhausted, it had been a long day, but it was worth it. All of the effort in rehab. All of the struggles to walk, to eat, to sleep, to survive—it was worth it. It felt as if I was climbing a mountain and finally starting to reach the summit.

The bronchoscope wasn't bad at all. It was odd getting hooked back up to lots of monitors. Doing this in the hospital brought back lots of memories. The doctor took a small snippet of the lung to evaluate. There was no evidence of cellular rejection, and all of the fungal smears came back negative. Everything was just fine. We were so relieved that we got out of town for a weekend on the beach. It was the first real time I had slept anywhere but my house or the hospital since the previous August. For me, this was not normal. It was a tad unnerving, but actually putting my feet in the sand almost brought me to tears. I never thought I'd see the ocean again, yet here I was. The weather was spectacular, the company was wonderful, and things were looking up. I still had to plan around my medicine regimen and my twice daily vital sign checks, but that didn't matter. Knowing what is expected makes doing that thing attainable. It also helped me understand that as I progressed, I would have to ask more questions and plan ahead even more than I had in the past, if that were even possible.

June

Things are going to be different from here on out. We are moving past the daily ins and outs of the physical healing that was still taking place. In fact, things were progressing such that, for the most part, I was starting to move on from worrying about my physical status. What was now starting to be front and center was the mental aspect of my healing. I'm not sure I fully realized it, but this would be a far greater challenge. As the world began to open back up post COVID (sort of) and we started to see more people, I was starting to get the common question-"How are you feeling?" How do I answer this? What is the right answer? To say that I felt "fine" or "OK" or "good" seemed trite and almost undersold the whole thing. Slowly, the "right" answer started to become clear. I started to tell folks, "I am just now physically able to start healing mentally." For the first three months post transplant, the entire healing process had been focused on my physical needs. Those were now starting to dissipate and I was turning a bit more inward on my healing. It was a turn that would prove challenging and lonely.

Our family had weathered a hell of a year. A line from a Jason Isbell song kept running through my head: "Last year was a son of a bitch for nearly everyone we know." A true statement to be sure, but it felt as if we had been through a bit more than most. Everyone's thing is their thing and nobody's issues are any greater or less than anyone else's, I guess. It's simply … theirs. And the thing is, everyone has to process their thing the best way they can and they need the space and allowance to do just that. As for our house, we had survived a year of COVID, remote learning, a return to school, birthdays in isolation, holidays in isolation, a never-ending tax season, my stuff, and Emma graduating high school. It was a bit much, but somehow we made it. I guess the strategy of putting one's head down and pushing forward had worked. But at what cost?

By all rights, I should've been dead. It's hard to write those words. It's even harder to accept them. Back in January/February I don't think I was ready to accept where I was in my journey. I was so focused on what I could control that I couldn't confront my potential death. I asked Erin if she knew I was as sick as I was. Her look said it all. As it turns out, everyone around me had accepted the fact that I was deathly sick. For me, I was just trying to get by. Looking back on it now, I don't know how I did it. I would see family or friends rarely. My girls would stop and check on me but I spent the majority of my time alone in my room. I felt very lonely and I would stay lonely even when in the hospital surrounded by people. As my physical healing progressed post transplant, I still wasn't dealing with the whole "nearly dying" thing. I was so focused on clinic visits and getting my strength and stamina back that I was suppressing the mental healing I needed. It was easier to take a walk around the block and do some light weights than it was to give in to a bit of introspection. Now, however, that physical part was getting easier and I'd have no choice but to start to address my mental state.

It was a weird juxtaposition of emotions. June 4 was Rachel's 15th birthday, and I was thrilled to be able to take her to the DMV to get her driver's permit. I was elated to be able to be a part of her celebration. I was happy to be at her party with a few of her friends and to laugh with them as they enjoyed each other's company. I was content with the joy these teenagers were showing and the way they found fun in the simplest parts of the day. Watching them trying to hit golf balls and evaluating the taste of various ice creams was pleasant and it reminded me of why I fought. Her birthday was the start of a big week in our house. She turned 15 on a Friday, and the following week was all about Emma graduating high school. Because of the pandemic, everything was different than in years past. Her Senior Assembly would be held at the stadium, and the class would be split in half. We were provided tickets so that Erin and I could be there along with one grandparent from each side. On Thursday of that week, graduation was to be held in the same location and the same manner, though we had tickets for the three of us and for all four grandparents. In true Class of 2021 fashion, the weather forecast called for rain. The Class of '21 had to have been the most flexible group of high school seniors ever. At the last minute, the graduation ceremony was moved inside into the gym and the class was split into fourths. I applauded the school for this as it allowed all of us to attend, and we managed to secure another ticket that allowed Erin's sister to attend, as she had flown in from Florida for the festivities. I didn't cry at the ceremony, even if I did get a little misty. I was so proud of my daughter. I was proud of what she had faced and overcome. I was proud to be there.

My family would come to roll their eyes at this statement: "Guys, I should be dead." I think they rolled their eyes to keep their emotions in check. At least that's what I'm telling myself. The thing is, I *was* supposed to be dead. There was no rational explanation for my being there other than that I got lucky. That was the range of emotions—you see? Inside my head I was so happy to be alive and to be a part of these milestones in the lives of my daughters. Yet there was this little nagging voice that said, "Dude, you should be dead." It was a rollercoaster and the ride was never ending. When I worked at Disney World back in 1997 we rode a particular ride one night near closing time. We knew the cast members working the ride and they permitted us to stay on it and to ride it multiple times in a row. It must have been five or six times in a row that we looped the ride. We knew the ups and downs, we knew the songs, we knew the whole ride. But we stayed on. This was the life I was currently living. I was on the same ride day in and day out, but I had no desire to get off of the ride. It was finally starting to be worth enjoying again.

I was surrounded—by the friends of my girls, by family, and by our friends. Yet I was alone. This is where it gets hard for me. I missed being around people, but I couldn't stand to be around them at the same time. My mind was a muddled mess and it was hard to process everything going on.

I was on a road that no one understood. No two people process events the same way. Even if they went through the same trauma, how they frame it and deal with it will be different. It's based on so many outside factors, so how could it not be? It seemed to me that this was why the doctors were so focused on measurable and clinical data. They were not prepared to deal with the emotional aspect of the journey. That, and the measurements were kind of important in keeping me alive. The social worker was useless at helping emotionally, and the psychologist had been absent in my healing. My personal therapist, as good as she was, could offer little in terms of support. It was becoming clear to me that I was gonna have to face this on my own. Even other transplant recipients would be little help to me. I had been such an outlier that I had little in common with those around me. I was younger, got sicker faster, got listed quickly, and got transplanted in a hurry. My time in the hospital was short, with little in the way of complications, and my time at rehab was short too. While it was true that for some I was an inspiration, I didn't want that. It was nice that others looked at me as what "could be." But, I didn't want them looking at me and expecting the same results. I didn't want them to get their hopes up that their story would look like mine. Though we were on similar paths, we were all treading ground that no one else had walked. We could listen to each other, but our points of view were different, and that impacted our healing.

I had a physical therapist tell me at my last appointment that I had been that rare patient. I had come to physical therapy ready to do what I needed to do to get out of there as quickly as possible. She told me that she had once had a patient who took a year to clear rehab because he simply refused to do the work. See? Similar paths, different routes. All of my efforts had been focused on getting well enough to be a part of all of the events that June brought, and I succeeded. What was next? My life was starting to be filled more with questions than answers. I was having to confront the fact that my life was now going to progress differently than I thought. What of the old me was left? What was the new me supposed to be? How was I supposed to get there? Where even was "there"?

I often found myself crying. It would happen for no apparent reason and at no logical time. It was as if my mind was operating independently from my body. There were times when the tears were simply unavoidable. It followed a very predictable pattern. Someone would ask me how I was. I'd answer. Sometimes, they'd follow up with this gem:

"How does it feel knowing someone had to die for you to get those lungs?"

Holy shit. How in the hell do you answer that? There is absolutely no "right" way to answer that question. It was in trying to answer it that I would find myself getting teary-eyed and emotional. I had been struggling with how to come to grips with this part of the process from the beginning. When I was waiting, I felt like a ghoul. I knew that for me to have a chance someone else had to lose their life. I had sunk to a place where icy roads were exciting because they might lead to a car wreck that could lead to lungs. I'd hear a medical helicopter overhead and I'd wonder what the blood type of the patient was. I felt terrible. But I felt like I did. It was horrible, but I justified it. Then the call came for me, and I knew that someone had died. There was a family in absolute turmoil and their loss was to be my gain. How does one even attempt to make sense of this? Give and take, life from death. It was irrational and just too much to process then. The only thing I found out concerning my donor was their age. 27. The person was 27 at their death. I was 44. A 27 year old with a family, with people who loved them, with hopes, with dreams, with a life ahead of them, was gone. My middle-aged self was getting another shot. It wasn't fair, but that's what it was. Unlike cancer treatments or some other transplants, for me to keep going, someone else's time had to be up. I tried to make it make sense by telling myself that I didn't know them. I didn't cause their death. They had signed up to be a donor. All of that was hollow. All of it was a way to push dealing with it down the road. Erin tells folks that after my first trip to Cuba, I came back with my mind a mess. I had seen things and had experiences that really rocked me to the core. I was charged up with making a change. I thought I could single-handedly bring down a government and bring freedom to my friends there. Obviously I couldn't do any of that. What I could do was take Spanish lessons so on my next trip I'd be able to talk with my friends and engage in simple communication. I could do what I could. So it was with this. I was charged up. I wanted to reach out to the donor family, I wanted to do so much. What I could do was to live in a way that would honor the sacrifice of the donor. I could make sure that I treated our lungs with the respect they deserved. I could keep them healthy. I could exercise them. I could protect them as best as I could. I could continue to experience my life. Hopefully, in some small way, I could make their death have meant something. I'm sure that to their family that would be of little solace, but it was all I could do. And thinking about it made me cry.

I had settled into a routine by this point. I was up most mornings before the sun, usually after a fairly restless night. I would take my first walk of the day and really push it to work my entire cardiovascular system. I wanted to stretch those lungs and make them breathe. I'd make sure I was done in time to take my medicines at 7:30 a.m. as instructed. After that, I would do some light weights a couple days a week. Mornings were spent writing and afternoons playing some guitar. I'd go for another walk with Erin in the evening and then cook dinner. After dinner, it was time for my 7:30 p.m. meds and then time to start getting ready for bed. It doesn't seem like much in hindsight, but it required stamina and strength to get though the day. I was also able to start assuming more of a helping role at the house. Now that I could drive, I was able to take Rachel to appointments or the pool. I could help with some grocery runs and even do light housework. It felt good to be able to start contributing once again. For so long I had felt so useless, it was nice for that to start to disappear. One of the hardest things for me in this journey was not being useful and needing so much help with everything.

When I was at my sickest, all I could do by myself was use the bathroom and shower. Even those two simple tasks were almost too much for me. It was hard to go from being as active as I was to being so reliant on others. Now, I had started to reassume my position as a contributor in the family. For me, this felt like another step toward normalcy. Being able to take some of the household burdens off of Erin was satisfying. Since I could no longer work, at least now, this was a way to add some value to the family.

To look at me, you wouldn't know that I had anything going on from a health standpoint. At least with my shirt on. Once the shirt came off, woo boy. It got funny going to the beach and the pool and seeing people stare at my scar. I thought about charging a fee to take a look. That was the visible scar. My emotional scars were invisible but deeper. I knew that I would be dealing with the physical healing for quite some time and that the scars would be there forever. My sternum was still sore and I was convinced that I would be sore there for the foreseeable future. I found myself looking in the mirror with my shirt off frequently, and it wasn't to admire the fine specimen of manhood looking back at me. I would look at myself and run my hand along my scar; I'd feel the bumps and ridges; I'd feel my sternum where the wires had held my chest together; I'd notice that my chest was a little uneven now, and I could understand how people would stare. I was staring as well, but I was in awe. I can't imagine what someone going through cancer treatments endures with hair loss. I can only project that some of their emotions mirrored those I had. I would stare at myself and wonder just how in the hell I had gotten to this point in my life. Sometimes I'd see my face in that reflection and see remnants of the boy and young man I had once been. Sometimes, I saw the face of a middle-aged man who had been through the wringer. No matter who was staring back at me, we were all confused.

I was confused for one simple reason—for the life of me, I couldn't figure out why this had happened to me. I am fully aware that everyone goes through struggles, and health issues are not unique to me. But why? I felt that between the rheumatoid arthritis and the celiac, I had been given enough to deal with, yet here I was. I'm sure there are other medical procedures and recoveries that are more difficult, but be damned, hadn't I been given enough? I was beginning to spend too much time looking at the why part of the equation. It started to dawn on me that it really didn't matter why this had happened to me—it just *had*. I can't believe that others facing their own crises don't have the same thoughts. There comes a point where focusing on the why starts to be detrimental to the mental healing. I had reached that point. To be sure, I was still confused, yet it was time to push that behind me. My illness would be part of my past, my surgery and time in the hospital were starting to be memories, and those first months of healing were gone. It was time to stop looking in the rearview mirror and begin to focus on what lay ahead of me. My past was just that: my past. I had no idea how to move forward. I didn't know what to be anymore. The self I was had disappeared forever. I had started to come to grips with some of the mental challenges of the transplant. I was now trying to figure out what the rest of my life was supposed to be. At least I had a life to think about.

As grateful as I was for this chance, I was still dealing with feelings of anger and sadness. I was angry that I was having to go through this entire ordeal. It felt unfair and I was having lots of difficulty making sense of the whole thing. I was looking at my life and I just couldn't get out of my own head. At times, the anger was preventing me from truly engaging in my life. It felt like I was in a continual slow simmer. It felt like the smallest little thing would set me off, and it sometimes did. My anger that flashed at my family was misplaced. I was mad at my situation, not them. But how do you express anger at a situation? How could I be angry at what truly bothered me? It felt like an impossible task. As a result, it was my family that had to bear it. It was unfair and it was all on me. I would have to develop strategies to effectively address my anger. That would come with time. It would get easier, but it would never get easy.

The sadness was another emotion that I wasn't expecting. In addition to being almost constantly angry, I was almost always sad. It's true that I was happy and grateful to be living and a part of my family, but there was also a tinge of sadness in everything. I was sad for what I had lost and that there were things that I would no longer be allowed to do. Every transplant clinic has their list of do's and do nots, and mine was no different. It was just hard facing that list. I was going to need to figure out a new way of living. That, too, would come with time. It's just hard in to figure out a new you your mid 40s. I understand that everyone goes through changes in different stages of their lives. It just felt like all of my changes were forced on me. I didn't ask for any of this, yet I was having to figure it out. I needed to be given the space and grace to become whatever the new version of me would be.

One thing that was abundantly clear to me as I began to plot out my future was that I would no longer put off things for the future. None of us are guaranteed any moment other than the one we are in right this second. I mean, this may be the last thing you ever read. If that's the case, I hope you don't regret that decision. After facing such a life-changing event, I was a little more in tune with trying to focus on the present. At Emma's graduation ceremony, I didn't take a single photo. For me, it was more important to be present in that moment. To fully be there. To watch her face, to see her smile, to hug Rachel when she cried. Maybe this is why I faced this challenge? Was it to get me to be more attuned to the here and now? If so, it was working. Others could take pictures. Whenever I want to, I can close my eyes and be back in that gym surrounded by family and see Emma. I can feel Rachel place her head against me seeking some solace. I could be a dad. I like to think that my donor is somewhere where they can see this and it makes them smile.

When I speak of putting off things, I don't simply mean big things like vacations or major events like that. I'm talking of the little things too. Dinner with my family. Driving Rachel somewhere. Being available to listen to Erin after work. Activities that used to be annoyances or distractions were now small blessings. As these last few months of us all being at home together were passing, these small moments were even more important. I was still on a rollercoaster of emotions. I found myself getting aggravated with small things. The lows were pretty low, but the highs were pretty high. Fortunately, the highs were starting to win out. I wonder, dear reader, if you see a pattern emerging in my story? Do you see that so much of what I am describing and speaking of centers around me taking care of others? Is this my role? Is my purpose moving forward to be at the disposal of others? What about my wants? What about my needs? So many people seemed to assume that now that I had received the lungs, my needs and wants had been covered. I should be satisfied with where my life was. Umm, no. Yes, I was grateful for the lungs. The lungs, in my view, were a necessary tool to continue my life story. Here we are again at the same inflection point. What is that story?

My future. Wow. How to address that little question? I think all of us struggle with trying to become the person we think we should be. I think becoming who we are meant to be is hard for most of us. Very few people just "know" who or what they are to be. All of us go through metamorphoses in our lives. Who I was a kid or even a young man is different from who I am now. This is true for all of us. Events in our lives change us. It's only natural for this to be the case. I have to tell you, having a double lung transplant really throws a wrench in any plans you might have. I've said that the biggest mistake I made professionally was leaving the classroom. Since that point I had struggled to find happiness in a job. I had moments of joy in work since then, but they had been fleeting, and the unhappy times at work had sadly outweighed the happy times. In the fall of 2019, Erin came to me and told me to figure out what I wanted to do and to "blow up my life and start something new." She has since told me that I took her suggestion to "blow up my life" a little too far, but then I've never been known for doing things halfway. Most would just quit their job and start something new. Not me … no … I had to be the one to get a life-threatening disease in the middle of a pandemic. I had made the decision that working in the medical field could be an interesting way to pass a few years, so I figured I'd go get a certification in doing x-rays. I thought that given my time being x-rayed for my RA, this was something I could do. It's funny looking back, but I had absolutely no idea just how much experience in radiology I would get!

As 2020 began, I completed the prerequisites to apply to the local community college for their program. I took a nurse's assistant class (information that would be useful), a math class (because it had been more than 10 years since I took math—had it changed?), and an anatomy and physiology class (the unit on the respiratory system came in handy). I submitted all of my paperwork for admittance to the cohort set to begin in January of 2021 and waited. And then things got weird. When I got my acceptance letter, I had to turn down my spot. My pulmonologist basically told me that I needed to give up on that idea. It's not that I was in love with the idea, but I had put in the work and felt like I had a direction forward. Not only that, but he said I should apply for Social Security Disability Insurance. Well, damn. It was almost like he said, "It's cute you had a plan, but I'm going to need you to cancel those ideas and any ideas you have about working at all for the future." Other changes would have to be made in my daily life if I got the transplant. At this point, it was up in the air.

Well, that was then. Way back in September when we thought medication might help. Now, we had traveled a road that led through transplant-land and to life afterwards. I was now facing the dilemma of "what's next" again. I was alive and facing the uncertainty of how to move on daily. Fine, then, what to do? I still don't know. And that is OK.

———

My journey is far from over. At least, I hope that to be the case. For all of us the future is uncertain. I realize that I am not unique in not being sure what lies around the corner. I think what makes my story a little different is that I am happy to have a corner to turn. I'm slowly beginning to come to grips with the entire mind-warp this has been. I have found comfort and healing in looking at the photos from my surgery. There is something oddly healing about seeing those pictures. There is one of me prior to being placed under anesthesia. I remember them taking that photo and wondering if that would be my last picture. Now, I can look at it and grin. It was the last picture of a sick me. Looking at the photos of my old lungs resembling burnt beef brisket, and being able to say good-bye to them is an odd thing to confront, but it is healing. Seeing the photo of my new lungs as they prepare to place them in my body after looking at the old lungs never fails to fill me with gratitude. The hardest pictures to look at and to process are the photos that show my exposed chest cavity. I know that looking at the inner workings of the human body is not something everyone can stomach. For me, I am glad to have a picture. It is a reminder of what my body went through just so I could get one more day. It also provides me a chance to be a little more forgiving with myself. My body had been through hell and had come out of the other side. It was a reminder to me that if my body could come out, so could my head. I just needed to be patient. Plus, how many people do you know can show a photo on their Apple Watch or iPhone of their chest cavity? It's pretty rad and quite the ice breaker. Whenever I meet someone new, boy do I have a story to share. My "two truths and a lie" turn will be hard to decipher!

Our lives are slowly returning to whatever normal passes for here in our little corner of the world. That seems to be the greatest gift of all. After all of the emotions of the past year and particularly the past five months, it has been nice to start to fall back into routines. I no longer need around-the-clock watching. I can drive. I can contribute. I can do things. But. But something still nags at me.

Everyone around me seems to have a plan for their future. Emma is heading off to college and I am thrilled for her. She has worked hard and deserves her shot. I am also slightly jealous of her. I remember those heady days before moving in to Morrison Dorm on South Campus all those years ago. I remember the excitement of my first football game, my first classes, my first of everything in Chapel Hill, and I am excited that she will soon have those experiences in Greenville. As excited as I am for her, I am sad she is leaving. I am sad to not see her every day and be part of her daily life. As with everything on this journey, I am trying to find balance in my excitement and sadness. It is a constant struggle.

Rachel is moving through high school in remarkable fashion. She crushed her freshman year, participated in ways I never imagined, and made some friends. She is focused on being more involved in the coming years and has started to consider her options for college. I had always envisioned her more as the "Ferris Bueller" of the family, traveling outside of the box post–high school. Ultimately, I don't care. Her future is hers to write and she has started off quite well. As for Erin, she keeps right on clicking with her business. It's growing, and I am proud of what she and her business partner have built from scratch. To be sure, there are headaches with owning a business, but so far, the good has outweighed the bad.

Yet again, we face the same problem. Everyone has a plan. Everyone but me. I've been told that I should be grateful that I have a future. That now I can look to the future. I know this to be true and don't get me wrong—I am grateful for the chance. The issue is that it is sometimes hard to really be happy about the future when so much of it is uncertain. So much of "Old Ronald" is gone. Because of the lungs, I now have additional food restrictions. Some of them will be gone within a year, but some will be lifelong. Not that this is a is a huge deal. Fresh fruits and vegetables will return soon enough, and I particularly look forward to fresh pineapple and salads again. Raw seafood is gone forever. Oh, well. I don't love sushi and raw oysters enough for it to matter. Maybe that is the secret to figuring out all of this. Perhaps I need to start looking at what will return? I can't swim in freshwater bodies of water anymore due to the risk of bacteria. This makes me sad. But, to be completely honest, I am starting to get a little old to do some of the things I used to do anyway. Things that are now a no-go. It probably wouldn't be wise to rope swing into rivers in Jamaica even if I hadn't had a lung transplant. At my age, I'd probably hurt myself. The good news is that I can look back at pictures or recall the memories of having done that in the past. Times spent with my girls when they were younger and I was too. Now,

I'll be the guy holding the bag while everyone else rides the roller coaster. I'm OK with that too. They were starting to become painful. So it's just a new normal for me. I suppose I am fortunate that all of this happened when my girls were older and we had already done so much together. I am proud of our parenting strategy of focusing on experiences over things. Wait—is that a nugget of wisdom? I think it is. Things come and go. Our latest device or car or whatever is obsolete almost as soon as we buy it. What never becomes obsolete are the memories I have of time spent with my family. Recalling various trips or events or experiences shared got me through lots of tough times this year. Even now, as we create new memories, old ones are never really that far away. And even when I am gone (many years from now) my girls can remember those times, and I'll still be there.

What I am looking for in my life is something that will light a fire in my gut. Something that exhilarates me. Something that really fires me up. Music does that. Travel does that. At least while I'm listening or on a trip. I need to work harder to find those little moments in my daily life. I can't always be on a trip or at a show. I have to be able to find it closer to home. The issue is that the goalposts have moved. Little things that used to do the trick seem to be a little "less-than" these days. Once you have stared at death and come out the other side, your "excite-o-meter" tends to shift. I suppose I need to recalibrate it and bring it more in line with norms. The world often paints an unattainable picture of what we are supposed to use as our basis for normal. I need to spend a little more time in my own head and figure out what my normal is. Maybe it's something wild and crazy. Maybe not. Maybe it's a combination of the two and I have to continue to strike that balance. Who knows, maybe learning to relinquish some control of my life and working to find a new balance is the great lesson in all of this. Maybe there is no lesson, I just had to endure.

My future is blank. I will keep finding new ways to fill my days and challenge myself intellectually. That's exciting. For so much of my life,— OK, all of it—I had been so focused on what came next. What this whole experience has taught me is that I need to be content in the now. That in no way means I can't look forward to things, only that I need to happy with the moment I have right in front of me. For far too long in my life, I was so preoccupied with moving to the next step, I lost sight of that. I regret that. I regret that I can't recall certain things in my girls' lives. I regret that I didn't take advantage of conversations with older members of my family. I regret that I was trying to speed through my life. What was my damn hurry? Where was I trying to go? All of us have such a finite period of time on the planet, and here I was trying to rush through my time like I was watching a bad TV show. I hadn't asked for this reality but here it was. It was a chance to refocus and figure myself out. That is the biggest gift of all. My new lungs had given me a chance to refocus my entire worldview. Yes, it's true I was still a little impatient. Yes, people still aggravate me a little. Yet small pleasures seemed bigger. I was starting to appreciate the small gifts on my morning walks. I said good morning to rabbits for crying out loud. I appreciated the smell of a freshly watered lawn. I was thrilled to see an albino deer. All of that happened on one walk. Can you believe that? On one walk, I had all of those experiences. Experiences that in the past I would've cruised on by and probably not had.

Since I had gotten so sick, I was so completely focused on trying to get through a day and survive. We were all living day-to-day. And now. Now, my story can continue. I can plan trips for my family. I can look to a future with Erin. I don't know how long that future will be. I hope "we'll get 40 years together," as the Jason Isbell song goes, but I do know that for however long I get with her, I will work to make memories. Rachel will only be home a few more years and then she will set off on her own adventures. As I sit here, right now, I am content. My future, which such a short time ago was in doubt, is now spread before me. We have experiences planned for the next few months. I have to keep working on my healing, but I also get to do that. That in itself is a victory.

It's hard writing the end of a story that is still being written. By all rights, I should be dead. Wrapping my head around that simple fact is not an easy task, but I am getting used to it. The very fact that I am not dead is truly amazing. It is a testament to the hard work and expertise of many people. It is a testament to the selflessness of the donor. It is a testament to the love and support of my family. It seems like my role is in this whole thing was to get sick. I do what I can to get better, and physically, that continues. The mental part falls to me and me alone. I am trying to stretch my legs and regain some of my life. I've mentioned repeatedly the healing power of music. I believe in this power. Everyone has something that they cling to, I suppose. Part of my healing is starting to get back into the world, and recently I was able to attend a small concert. It was a reduced capacity, intimate show with one of my favorite performers. If you don't know Cory Branan, you should. His ability to turn a phrase resonates with me deeply. At this show, I was able to thank him for what his music has meant to me through my challenges. I'm used to bringing people to tears, but this time it hit a little harder when I made him tear up. At this particular acoustic show, I was particularly impacted by some of his words. In his song "Imogene" he sings, "We've got to act on the embers / ash won't remember the way back / to fire." I once had a fire burning in me. Over time, that fire has died out and in some ways, a part of me will never come back. I guess that part of me is ash and those black lungs represent that in a way that I will always remember, but I still have embers in me. That's what I need to act on. I now have the breath needed to get those embers to relight and return to fire.

I'll figure out what my next step is. My life begins again. Next steps begin each and every day and for that I am grateful. I am not the only person to do it, but I faced death down and won. This time, at least. My revelations are not that earth shattering. I have not gone through anything that others have not faced. But, this was my experience. It was hard. It was scary. I almost lost everything. But I am still here. I don't know for how long—none of us do. But what I can tell you is that once you have faced death, there is an urgency about each day that those who haven't faced it don't fully understand. You feel the need to maximize each and every experience and you feel a little disappointment in each day that doesn't feel maximized. It's a fine line. You want to be grateful to be here, and you are, but you want to do stuff. Whatever your stuff is. Erin and I talked about this recently. I told her how important it was to me to truly experience my life with whatever time I had left. I don't want to put off for years things that I can experience now. Trying to find balance in life is more important than ever. Maybe that has been the lesson in all of this, if there is a lesson at all. This past year has taught us all how crucial learning to live in balance is to all of us. Finding balance in our work, our families, and making sure to care for ourselves is more challenging than ever. But never has it been more important. Knowing how hard this is, I wish you all luck.

So that's it. That's my story. At least for now. If you made it this far with me, I truly thank you. If you were part of this journey, I'll never be able to thank you enough. I will never be able to put into words my level of gratitude for the medical professionals who kept and continue to keep me alive. There is no way I can tell my family what they have meant to me in this process. Every time I try to tell them, I come to tears and I can't get it out. It is impossible to tell them how much their love and support has meant and how it kept me alive. There were times that were very dark in this journey. There were days filled with hope. They were my constant, and they kept me going. I love them more than I can say. I have no words. Each day, I hope to do right by my donor. I never fail to remember the sacrifice of their family and how careful I need to be of the gift I received. I want my life to be a testament to that person, whoever they were. I want to honor them. It seems to me that the way to do this is to live each day to the fullest. To laugh, to learn, to love, and to cry a little each day. If I can do that, I'll have done something. Just a few months ago, my life was being lived on a minute-to-minute basis. Now I have months, and hopefully years, spread before me. I am excited for what those days hold. I am not expecting every day to be free of problems. I will face challenges, of this I have no doubt. That's what life is. And you know what? After facing this, my family can face anything. We can stare down any challenge and meet it. There's nothing left to write now.

Wait—there is one last thing to tell you, and I can't emphasize this enough. Hug your loved ones. Every single chance you get. In a life full of experiences, hugs are some of the best. I've gotten lots of hugs lately. Each one is special. If you see me around, expect a hug. I'm really starting to dig them.

Acknowledgements

First of all, to my family. Without my three girls I wouldn't have survived this ordeal. To Erin, Emma, and Rachel-Thank you. To all of my family, thank you for the support. Thank you for checking in on me, visiting, and driving to and from physical therapy. Thank you to the doctors, nurses, etc. at UNC. There are simply too many of you to name but every one of you was key to my survival. Special thanks to Dr. Leonard Lobo, Dr. Raymond Coakley, and Dr. Benjamin Haithcock. Thanks to my editor, Henry Gifford. To all of you who brought my family meals and tried to keep their spirits afloat, thanks. Tupper, Lynda, Debra, Neil, Chip, William, Ed, and the rest of my friends-Thank you. Now-let's get to livin'....